Home in Fenwick

Books by Author

The Playmakers (with **Arthur** Cantor)

Off-Broadway

Enter Joseph Papp

After the FACT

Home in Fenwick

Memoir of a Place

Stuart W. Little

iUniverse, Inc.
New York Lincoln Shanghai

Home in Fenwick
Memoir of a Place

Copyright © 2008 by Stuart W. Little

All rights reserved. No part of this book may be used or reproduced by any means, graphic, electronic, or mechanical, including photocopying, recording, taping or by any information storage retrieval system without the written permission of the publisher except in the case of brief quotations embodied in critical articles and reviews.

iUniverse books may be ordered through booksellers or by contacting:

iUniverse
2021 Pine Lake Road, Suite 100
Lincoln, NE 68512
www.iuniverse.com
1-800-Authors (1-800-288-4677)

Because of the dynamic nature of the Internet, any Web addresses or links contained in this book may have changed since publication and may no longer be valid.

The views expressed in this work are solely those of the author and do not necessarily reflect the views of the publisher, and the publisher hereby disclaims any responsibility for them.

ISBN: 978-0-595-43938-6 (pbk)
ISBN: 978-0-595-69231-6 (cloth)
ISBN: 978-0-595-88261-8 (ebk)

Printed in the United States of America

For my grandchildren, Melissa, Jonathan, and Eliza

Contents

Acknowledgments ix
Chapter 1:   "Going Down to Fenner" 1
Chapter 2:   Founding Fenwick 10
Chapter 3:   Early Days 16
Chapter 4:   Wreck Buoy, Lighthouse, and Home 22
Chapter 5:   Nineteen Thirties 32
Chapter 6:   Greener Fields 42
Chapter 7:   Hartford and Hepburn 51
Chapter 8:   After the War 60
Chapter 9:   Apart from Fenwick 75
Chapter 10: Forsaking Fenwick for the South of France 97
Chapter 11: "Suffer the Little Children" 109
Chapter 12: Newcomers Arriving 116
Chapter 13: Through the Sixties 124
Chapter 14: On the Water 141
Chapter 15: Home Improvements 151
Chapter 16: Rushing through the Nineteen Nineties 164
Chapter 17: Departure 175
Postscript: Alive in Fenwick 179

Acknowledgments

Discouragement as well as exhilaration are inherent in any writing project. I want to acknowledge a few of those who saved me from discouragement by reacting generously to the manuscript. My work might never have reached the stage of publication if my friends William and Caroline Zinsser had not given it its first reading and responded so warmly to it. I am indebted to them; to Anne Phelan for her rigorous and thoughtful proofreading at an early stage; to Thomas K. Carley for his wise, sympathetic, and closely annotated reading, and always and forever, to Anastazia for the kind of backing that keeps one going.

Chapter 1

"Going Down to Fenner"

"Going down to Fenner!" my father exclaimed, like a cheerleader to his cohorts, and we three children, my sister Virginia, my brother Ted, and I, climbed into the back of the LaSalle my father drove. Summer things packed, we headed down the road from Hartford for the fifty-mile trip to Fenwick and our cottage on the shore. Under his coaching, we looked out for such familiar landmarks as Bible Rock and the fearful, grey granite jail in Haddam. We gripped the edge of our seats when he slipped daringly out of gear for the long downhill slide from Middletown. My mother in front was a nervous passenger, and the long coast made her draw in her breath and protest. More relaxed in back, hardly questioning our father, we called out in unison the names of the river towns—Higganum and Haddam and Chester.

"Chester Gump!" exclaimed my father, summoning up the comic-strip character.

At Saybrook Point, the river came into view—the broad, shoaling mouth of the Connecticut River where it empties into Long Island Sound. The channel nun buoy leaned in the swift outgoing tide, tugging and twisting on its mooring chains. The familiar sea smells came in again.

As we turned the corner at Saybrook Point, we stared out the window at the town deaf and dumb man in his dusty black suit, high white collar, black derby, and scrubby beard, sitting mouth agape on the steps of Faulk's Store. Another year, and he was still there. We shuddered at seeing his dark silhouette on the steps of the store. Passing Faulk's, we reached the long causeway across South Cove, with the Sound beyond. The remembered marshy odor rose from the muck. "Low tide!" we sang out. The cottages of Fenwick appeared.

Our car came to rest on the dirt road ending at the waterfront. Long Island Sound spread out before us as far as we could see. "Blue sparkling Sound our childish eyes first knowing …," as the Fenwick Hymn has it, the hymn set to the melody of "Londonderry Air." In later years, we would sing it in the Fenwick chapel at the opening service of the summer and again, tearfully, at the closing service. "… Green meadows brightly decked with summer flowers."

The cottage, smelling of the sea, was musty from its winter hibernation, with cobwebs hanging in the corners. Nothing had been touched; the furniture was all in place, and the toys were in the cupboard. Last year's Fourth of July Stars and Stripes was still tipped in its jar on the fireplace mantle. All of summer lay ahead.

In those childhood years, Fenwick meant the cottage behind the clipped privet hedge, which was tall enough then to wall us in and ensure childhood privacy. Fenwick meant the house and its familiar rooms, the beach in front, and the Morrison boys next door, Gray and little Charlie. Later on, when we were up on bicycles, the place became a playground where one could run free from one end to the other, and no one's backyard was out of bounds for hide-and-seek or kick-the-can. Time was unlimited. The end of summer lay impossibly distant. A child could not believe in the end of summer. The openness of the place, the vastness of the sky, and the sea set one free. Still later, social conventions would crowd in, and the circle would widen. But the cottage remained the fixed point of reference to signify who we were.

In the afternoon, the gray moving van of Gould's Express would pull up in front of the cottage, and the men would unload the bikes along with some special pieces of furniture that had made the annual trip and the cases of clothes, including a stand-up trunk that carried our mother's summer dresses. Mrs. Thompson, a tall, dark-haired, handsome woman, who lived at the Point, would have cleaned the cottage, made the beds, and laid out the table silver. Behind her shimmering, steel-rimmed spectacles, she had a cheerful smile for us children. On the kitchen table, there was always a welcoming chocolate cake she had baked and a bowl of cherries. Her husband, Fred, was a carpenter and handyman from whom I learned painting shortcuts when he helped me work on our boat. For a time, he was employed in the borough as a guard. In the evening, he would patrol the borders of Fenwick holding the leash of his German shepherd.

The return to Fenwick would be repeated every year. Timeless and predictable, it was always something to look forward to, as reliable as our father's sure hand on the wheel of his car, something as certain as the tides and the turn of the seasons. We would be going back to Fenwick.

Our cottage was happily situated, on the front row with a full view of the Sound, yet far enough from the pier, the focal point of community activity, to be spared the heaviest traffic of dogs, baby carriages, children, grownups, bicycles, and, years later, golf carts. The principal converse of Fenwick, as it were, was a little out of earshot, and we were perfectly content to have it so.

House-proud Fenwick people had no doubt that their cottages were ideally positioned. We were sure of it too. We had the back lot giving us extra breathing room, and we felt less hemmed in by neighbors. When my father bought the cottage in 1920, when land was cheap, we also owned the lot immediately to the west, giving us a full Fenwick block. It was my father's conceit that he held this open space for reasons of personal privacy; when dressing in his western bedroom, he didn't need to draw the curtains.

Before his death in 1969, the west lot had been sold to a neighbor, Kay Marvin. She came from a moneyed Cleveland family, marrying into Hartford and Fenwick society. Her husband, Ed, had died on a family cruise. Kay continued bravely on with her husband lying refrigerated in the hold of the ship. Living one row directly in back of us, Mrs. Marvin wanted to safeguard her view of the water against possible construction in front. For a while, this gave my father a little cash in his pocket, fewer taxes to pay, and his privacy preserved at someone else's expense. To my father's surprise (he thought he had an understanding with Mrs. Marvin), she soon after sold her second-row cottage and built a modern, ranch-style brick house on our old waterfront lot. Completed before the creation of the Historic District Commission, which was formed to defend the design integrity of the community, the house was quite out of character with the shingled Victorian cottages of Fenwick with their wide porches, dormer windows, and angled roofs. We regarded it as a rude intrusion. Some years later, to screen off its offending, harsh white walls from our west porch, I planted a row of Canadian pines and olive trees.

Selling the west lot to Mrs. Marvin left three properties remaining in the family. Besides the back lot and the old house, which had been taken over by my family, my father and mother had bought the Clark cottage further up the beach. They retreated there in their latter years partly to remove themselves still further from the bustle of mainstream Fenwick but mostly out of the generous impulse to accommodate their children, freeing the old cottage for our use. In his gentle, generous way, my father had taken me aside one day and explained the move. He generally called my sister "sister" when he didn't call her Tib. "Sister and Charlie have a country house in Hartford, although they do like Fenwick. Ted and Sharon come to Little Haven, but they have a country house as well. You have only an apartment in New York." At my father's death, there was a piece of Fenwick for each of his three children. My older sister got the lot, expecting one day to build on it, my younger brother was allotted the Clark cottage, which they called "Little Haven," and I, luckiest of all, got the old house.

All the time I lived in New York, working as a reporter for a newspaper and at other writing jobs, Fenwick was the escape route from the clamorous city. If the city was harsh, Fenwick would be forgiving. Where the city was strange and alien, Fenwick was familiar, every path and hedge and lot, every expanse of beach and meadow. Fenwick was home.

Southeast View of the Cottage

Twenty-five years after the division of the properties, it was all gone. My sister had sold her property to me and my two eldest children. My brother had sold his house and moved inland to Old Saybrook. Then, in 1996, I sold my cottage, and the children and I sold the adjoining lot my sister had sold us in one package to one buyer.

Fenwick is on a narrow neck of land set apart from its mother town of Old Saybrook, like a piece of a jigsaw puzzle waiting to be connected. On the earliest charts, it is listed as Lynde's Neck, named after a seventeenth-century landholder. It takes its present name from Colonel George Fenwick who, in 1637, after the early English settlers defeated the Pequot Indians, became governor of the Saybrook Colony, which included the little peninsula that was named for him. Driving from Old Saybrook to the causeway at Saybrook Point, one passes Cyprus Cemetery, which holds a prominent sienna-colored gravestone ringed by a small, protective iron fence. Beneath this stone lie the bones of Lady Fenwick, who died in

1648. (In an open lot adjoining the cemetery is another historic stone, marking the founding on this spot of Yale University in 1701.)

West to east, Fenwick is a little less than a mile long, and no more than a third of a mile wide. Water surrounds it on three sides. To the north lies South Cove, a shallow, undredged body of water across which the causeway a third of a mile long leads from Saybrook Point to the partly obscured entrance to Fenwick. To the east is the wide mouth of the Connecticut River, which is guarded by the Inner Lighthouse, a tall, white-painted granite sentinel dating from 1838. The lighthouse is the top-selling postcard on the racks of the stationery and novelty stores in town. To the south, Fenwick faces the great sweep of Long Island Sound.

Originally cleared for farmland, the formerly flat and treeless Fenwick has undergone cosmetic change in recent years. Beginning in the late 1950s, volunteer tree wardens planted many varieties of trees and shrubs, particularly along the golf course. Added to the existing elms and tulip trees were rich stands of larches, maples, ashes, birches, white oaks, and black pines. Concerning this change, there were two schools of thought. One school applauded the transformation and extolled the beautification of Fenwick. The other, to which I subscribed, regretted the loss of the wild, spare look of the years before. It wasn't the Fenwick we knew in childhood.

Cottages are bunched in central Fenwick in three lines back from the shore. The largest and most impressive—our version of the Newport style—are oriented toward the pier where the swimmers and boaters congregate and where the social life of young mothers with babies is busiest. Laid out in 1896, the nine-hole golf course, a prominent geographical feature, exists without a country club. It winds its way through Fenwick behind and among the cottages, intruding on a number of backyards. Once as bare as any Scottish course, it remains today much as it was originally conceived, except for the trees and for some sophisticated changes in the construction, placement, and design of tee, trap, and green. The little chapel, St. Mary's by the Sea, is an unlisted hazard on the first hole.

The tennis courts are up from the pier on central Fenwick Avenue. This avenue was once the tar road leading from the old hotel, Fenwick Hall, to the water. Beyond the courts, to the east of the golf course, is another clump of cottages, once not regarded as Fenwick proper. Beyond them, the land falls off into a great, impenetrable salt marsh reaching to the river's edge. Then comes a final, smaller group of cottages lining the beach just west of the lighthouse breakwater—another part of Fenwick entirely.

What appealed to the original settlers is what appeals to the residents today: Fenwick's privacy, its cool summer breezes, its openness, and its long shoreline leading from cove to river to Sound. One friend of mine, never having visited Fenwick, called it "the enchanted kingdom," based on my description alone.

Katharine Hepburn, Fenwick's most famous resident, was a source of great pride. She embodied the spirit of the place too, having as a child and young adult, like the rest of us, learned all its sports and played all its games—and broken into empty houses, too, to explore. "Oh, I've been into that one," she would confess, looking around at cottages at our end of the beach. More than she defining Fenwick, Fenwick defined her. Later, she put Fenwick on the map, although more than one biographer has made the self-disqualifying error of mistaking Fenwick the place for the name of the Hepburn house. In later years, as her career lengthened and Kate mellowed, she was regarded as a national monument, assuming the regal status her fame entitled her to, and her house in Fenwick became a tourist attraction. Cars driving into Fenwick cruised slowly past the tennis courts to look down across the old fifth hole of the golf course at the Hepburn house on the water. And the guides of excursion boats from upriver, passing in front, can to this day be heard from shore, their voices amplified through megaphones carrying across the water on still days, announcing, "The white brick house on the shore is the home of Katharine Hepburn."

Katharine was both amused and appalled by this attention. "They say I have ruined Fenwick," she said, smiling, one day. She relished making trouble. A neighbor, bothered by the tourist traffic, called on her a number of summers ago. Rather boldly, I thought, he complained that an article about her in *Life* magazine and the pictures she allowed to be taken gave the place an undesired notoriety. It is doubtful that Miss Hepburn was much moved by this admonishment.

To her, as much as to any of us, especially in the later years of her life, this place was sacred ground. She protected her privacy with a large clumsily lettered sign at the entrance to her driveway reading, "Go Away Please." From her porch, she bellowed the same words, minus the "please," to anyone bold enough to cross the beach in front of her house in order to proceed down the shore. She was a film star who insisted on privacy for her family, which she defended fiercely; unlike many others in her profession, she had not felt obliged to obliterate her past in order to sustain the present image of her stardom.

"If I quit," she said one day when she was working on her last feature-length film *Grace Quigley*, "I'll go straight there and live in Fenwick. I don't care much for New York. I didn't care much for California either. I like the open country."

Her Hartford family were early cottagers. She excelled at all popular Fenwick sports—swimming, diving, sailing, tennis, and golf. At golf, she achieved nearly professional proficiency. Her lack of fear came from her mastery of all games. (She preferred to credit the teaching of her parents.)

A couple of times during the run of *Coco*, the 1969 musical about Coco Chanel, when Kate came to Fenwick on her Sunday off, my wife and I served as tennis partners for her and her brother Dick. At the outset of one match, Kate announced, "I'm not a coward, but if I'm at net and a ball comes at me, I'll turn away. I can't afford to be hit in the face while I'm in this play."

I made careful note not to hit to Kate at the net. It was a competitive match. It always was when a Hepburn faced you. So we played as hard as we could, and suddenly, I mis-hit a shot. The ball glanced off the rim of my racquet and went straight at Kate hitting her in the face. I was horrified. Luckily, she was all right and no damage was done to those famous cheekbones.

There was one other incident in that match. A group of young Fenwick kids, discovering who was on the court, drifted in and sat on the sidelines to watch. Slowly, a softly spoken chant began to arise from the crowd:

"Guess who's coming to dinner. Guess who's coming to dinner." Again, I was horrified for Kate. Paralyzed myself into speechlessness, I heard Kate take charge as only she could.

"Listen, kids," she said in an edgy Hepburn growl, taking a step or two towards the group, "just shut up or go away."

She was not an indignant movie star claiming privileges. It was if she half understood those children and might have recalled her own indiscretions as a kid growing up in Fenwick. The gang got to their feet and melted away.

In the end, we split sets and each walked away convinced we had won. After the match, we sat down on the steps of the nearest house and talked. The subject of sports injuries came up. Kate said, "You know, I can't remember a time in my life when I didn't wake up without some ache or pain."

Fenwick was the place Kate Hepburn left as a young girl when she was determined to have a career. Fenwick was the place she came back to, the place she was always leaving and was always returning to. Fenwick had a hold on all of us, but on none more than her. Once, on the Riverdale, New York, film set of *Grace Quigley*, she got in a car at midnight at the end of the work week to make the two-hour drive to Fenwick. She explained this nearly instinctive move as follows: "I would go there even if I could spend only an hour." I shared that compulsion. Fenwick was her permanent home, although it no longer was for me. Fenwick was the place she had chosen to live out the last years of her life.

When her busy film and stage career in Hollywood and New York was coming to an end, she said, "Someday, I think I'll awake in Fenwick and find that all that part of my life was just a dream."

Chapter 2

Founding Fenwick

Reminders of what Fenwick was like at its founding in the 1880s and 1890s lie all about us. The quarter-mile motor causeway across South Cove to the entrance of Fenwick was the very route of the Valley Railroad that was completed in 1871 and opened up Fenwick as a seaside summer resort.

From the causeway, looking east across the cove one can see the tops of the few remaining sea-worn pilings where seagulls and cormorants placidly sit. They mark the route of the carriageway that was erected to bring in building materials for Fenwick Hall, the hotel built at the time of the railroad's completion to be the centerpiece of the new resort.

Fenwick Hall stood on the rise of the road that leads into Fenwick where the flagpole now stands in a circular flowerbed. The three-story Victorian hotel with its grand porches and saltwater baths looked straight down Fenwick Avenue to the pier. The foundation of the pier itself, rebuilt in stone to replace the wooden structure, remains to this day. At the pier was the large pavilion of a bathhouse that is still vivid, at least in my memory, as that favorite playground for high-energy bicycle tag until it was washed away in the hurricane of 1938.

Fenwick Hall, however, was a little too grand for the Fenwick envisioned by its early settlers from Hartford—settlers bearing such Fenwick names as Bulkeley, Brainard, and Goodwin. Isolated as Fenwick was from the mother town of Old Saybrook by water on three sides, it valued its privacy, then as today, and was wary of outsiders. That wariness showed itself in a strong sense of protectionism and reserve, which seemed to be a characteristic of many of us at various times in Fenwick's history. We loved Fenwick too passionately to share its favors with others. We couldn't risk anyone upsetting an absorbing affair. A stranger coming into Fenwick was half expected to sign a non-disclosure agreement. Those early Hartford settlers had good reason to be upset when the notorious New Yorker Edward S. Stokes acquired Fenwick Hall at auction in 1889. His arrival is worth recounting because the event has parallels in the Fenwick of my time. Marion Hepburn Grant, younger sister of Katharine, tells the story in her indispensable 1974 book *The Fenwick Story* on which I have relied for early Fenwick history.

Stokes, in the oil business in Brooklyn, had business dealings with Jubilee Jim Fisk, who, with Jay Gould, controlled the Erie Railroad. Their relationship soured when Stokes took up with Fisk's mistress, the dark-haired beauty, Josie Mansfield. In the ensuing quarrel in 1872, when Fisk filed a lawsuit against Stokes, Stokes got out his revolver and killed Jubilee Jim Fisk on the staircase of the ladies' entrance to the Grand Central Hotel on lower Broadway.

He was sentenced to a remarkably short term of six years in Sing Sing and emerged after four years to start a new career as proprietor of Hoffman House on Broadway at Madison Square. Newly affluent, he arrived off Fenwick in 1889 in his black steam yacht *Fra Diavolo* and acquired the then nearly bankrupt Fenwick Hall at auction.

Stokes filled his hotel (and a few Fenwick cottages) with his New York cronies, fast-life figures from sports, stage, and politics. They included the Tammany Hall Democrat Boss Tweed, the Tammany-friendly judge Lester Holmes, the Republican police commissioner Jacob Hess, the actor Richard Mansfield and his lover Beatrice Cameron, and the magician Herrmann the Great—not an assortment likely to mix easily with the Hartford cottagers.

It was Stokes who paved Fenwick Avenue in tar. He rebuilt the pier in stone. He put up the grand pavilion. He laid tennis courts. But he did not last long in Fenwick. In July 1894, five years after Stokes acquired Fenwick Hall, the hotel was sold at auction for back taxes. And who acquired the hotel? None other than Fenwick's great patriarch, Morgan Gardner Bulkeley.

In 1917, however, as the United States entered World War I, the hotel unaccountably caught fire and burned to the ground. The cottagers were relieved. The circumstances were suspicious. It was suspected that someone prominent in Fenwick had touched the match to be rid of the place and, possibly, collect the insurance. In my day, Jack Davis, who was in his nineties, had our longest memory. He was still shaking his head over this long-forgotten event, wondering who was responsible.

The name of Bulkeley threads through the whole history of Fenwick even to the present day. A passenger on the first downriver run of the Valley Railroad in 1871 was Eliphalet A. Bulkeley, founder of the Aetna Life Insurance Company. He was the father of Morgan Gardner Bulkeley, the key and essential figure in the evolution of Fenwick and Fenwick's most distinguished name. He was the reason my father came to Fenwick and our family settled there in 1920.

Governor Bulkeley practically owned Hartford at the turn of the century. He was a large man—in spirits, physique, and mind. He was rich and politically powerful. In addition to being related to the financially astute Morgans and the land-rich Gardners, he was a veteran of the Civil War, having served in New York's Thirteenth Regiment; president of the Aetna Life Insurance Company after his father; and a prominent figure in politics successively holding office as councilman, alderman, and mayor of Hartford, governor of the state for two terms, and afterwards, United States senator.

He helped to organize the National Baseball League in 1876 and was its first president. A bronze relief of his rugged head with his distinctive handlebar moustache is in the National Baseball Hall of Fame in Cooperstown, New York.

Bulkeley served two terms as governor, the first by election, the second due to the extraordinary circumstances caused by an indecisive contest for the governorship in which neither of the two candidates (Bulkeley himself decided not to run) secured a majority and the legislature was deadlocked. In the interests of continuity, Bulkeley decided to remain in office. Finding the door to the governor's capitol office padlocked by the state's Democratic controller, Bulkeley called for a crowbar and forced his way into the office. He thereby earned the respectful epithet of "the Crowbar Governor." So he served out a second term in office.

Throughout his political career, holding office at local, state, and national levels, Governor Bulkeley remained president of Aetna Life. Once, in the state emergency caused by the above deadlock, he used company funds and his own wealth (later repaid in full) to finance the state government.

Forceful and decisive in state matters, he was also attentive to the affairs of Fenwick, which became a borough in 1899 and thereby enjoyed a number of self-governing privileges, including taxing power and zoning regulation. A hearty sportsman, he, together with a few associates, bought up New Saybrook Company land to create a golf course that wound its way through the borough. It is the second oldest golf course in the state.

He created Fenwick Hall, a privately held real estate entity, to retain strips of waterfront land, the commonly used pier, and other property, protecting the open integrity of the borough.

One day, seated comfortably on his porch, he watched a Pope-Hartford automobile chugging noisily down the slope on the road toward his house. As his influence enabled him to do, he thereupon arranged for the diversion inland, behind all of Fenwick, of a shoreline road ("Beach Road" on the ancient maps) that extended from the westernmost point of Fenwick to the lighthouse on the east, passing in front of the first line of cottages, including his own. For all time, this assured the front row of a view of the Sound unsullied by passing traffic.

On this ground alone, Governor Bulkeley, in addition to being a founding father, can be counted also as the patron saint of Fenwick. In high office, he looked after the people of Connecticut; in private life, he looked after his family and friends in Fenwick. And that chivalry of service, that obligation to one's own, extended down to his second son Houghton and his grandson Peter, both of whom served as wardens of the borough and preserved the place. Governor Bulkeley and Katharine Hepburn, together, in their different ways, were our inexhaustible symbols of excellence.

There was always a room for my father in the generous Bulkeley cottage, prominently placed with its wide-columned front porch in the first line of cottages near the pier. It was from here that my father first viewed Fenwick and sailed the Sound in his friend Morgan's graceful, gaff-rigged sloop *Petrel*. There, he fell in love with Fenwick. It was my father's fortunate friendship with Morgan Gardner Bulkeley that brought our family to Fenwick. When my father started out in business for himself, forming a company to manufacture brass plumbing goods, it was Morgan Gardner Bulkeley who came to his aid financially. He was repaid within a year. My father, throughout his life, remained grateful to the governor for his friendship.

We knew little of the history of that relationship. Still, it was revealed in small and subtle ways that were perceivable to us even as children. My father was not a deferential man, but in the loyalty he showed to the members of the governor's family—to Elinor and Houghton, his daughter and son, and to their children—we children sensed strong hidden connections that demanded our respect.

My father's loyalty was particularly evident in his relationship to the widow and three sons of his best friend, Morgan Gardner Bulkeley Jr., who died at the age of forty of a brain tumor. An exact contemporary of mine growing up, the youngest son, Ed, and I were members of the same Fenwick play class. We traded Saturday lunches presided over by our mothers back and forth in Hartford, followed one another to early schools and later to Yale, and remained lifelong friends. My son Christopher and his wife Betsy today are close friends of Ed's daughter and her husband.

Morgan Gardner Bulkeley died in 1922 at the age of eighty-four, still president of Aetna Life. In that same year, at the age of thirty-seven, my father became a director of the company and was the senior director at his retirement in 1959.

My father's position as a director of the city's most prominent enterprise gave him a standing that I gave little thought to growing up. It was never brought up at the dinner table. He never discussed it. Still, as the monthly meetings came up, one could sense my mother's pride in his position. Youth's thoughtlessness and a young man's ready dismissal of the achievements of a father of a different temperament are somehow tempered and altered in maturity and old age. "Honor thy father and mother" comes later in life. The small engraved silver pitcher given to my father when he retired as a director of Aetna today has a place at the top of my bookshelf.

My father, who was not rich, whose family was not prominent in the way of the Bulkeleys, who carried no worldly baggage but his character, was fortunate in his friendship with Governor Bulkeley. In 1920, assured of his welcome in Fenwick, he rented a small cottage by the golf course for his mother in her last years and the same year bought the cottage that became mine fifty-three years later.

Chapter 3

Early Days

Lying in bed at night gazing out of the second-story windows of the cottage at the dark, wide, mysterious Sound, I whisper to my sister. My sister, then about ten and nearly two years older, is in the bed next to me. Through our windows, we follow the lights of a passing boat far out in the water. The lights brighten first in one window, reappear in the second, and, some moments later, in the third, as the boat finally disappears on its unknown voyage to the west.

From our upstairs porch, we could look down the line of cottages to the pier and, still further beyond, to the lighthouse breakwater at the mouth of the river. Out at the end of the breakwater, as we lay in bed, we could see the Outer Light sweep its alternate beams of green and white into our bedroom, gleaming on the wall at the heads of the beds.

"Do you remember the stories we used to make up about the people on those passing boats?" my sister said one day. "How romantic they were!" On all those ships passing by our windows, we imagined the life and created the characters, usually as variations of our parents and their friends.

The ladies and gentlemen traveling on that boat bound for New York dressed for dinner and danced on the deck after dinner in the moonlight. They left their children behind in the care of nurses. Naturally, our passengers were rich, richer than our parents. And so were those people living in the grand houses we imagined to exist across the Sound, whose lights shone on the Long Island shore. They were a lot like our parents and their friends, only grander, more handsome, and beautifully dressed. Their houses surpassed our cottages in size and numbers of rooms.

Our bedroom faced south and opened on that upstairs porch to the east. On this porch, late on a Friday afternoon, my sister and I would be waiting, looking up the road to catch the first sight of our father's car as it turned the corner and approached the cottage. After sighting the car, we would race downstairs, the front screen door banging behind us, to be the first to greet him as he climbed out of the car to start his weekend. Coat slung over his arm, his sleeves rolled up after the baking drive down from Hartford, he would gather us up and begin his series of questions.

"Guess who I saw in town this week?" he would say. We would run through the usual suspects of Beatrix Potter characters.

"Was it Dr. Maggotty?"

"No."

"Was it Ribby?"

"No, it wasn't Ribby."

"Was it Cousin Tabitha Twitchit?"

"That's the one!"

It was always the last, of course. It was from this character that my sister came by her lifelong nickname of Tib.

It was a roomy old cottage. The east front porch of the house opened directly into our living room. Beyond was the dining room and beyond that the long west porch of the house where in good weather we always had our meals. In my parents' time, the porch had screens all along the waist-high rail. In my time, I had the porch redone with tall patio doors, and the porch remained the gloriously best part of the house, redeeming its more ordinary features. Upstairs, on the second floor, there were three other good-sized bedrooms. Our parents had the large west bedroom, which looked out on the adjoining lot between the Keeney cottage and us. They chose the west bedroom in order not to be awakened by the morning sun; the space of the lot assured them that extra measure of privacy my father enjoyed. There were two other bedrooms, one of which my sister moved into alone when we grew older. At the back of the house were three smaller bedrooms for our nurse, Margaret Donovan, and for the cook and maid. Years later, my wife and I cleared the back area of its dividing partitions and created one large bedroom for my son, Christopher, and his wife, Betsy, and a smaller, adjoining room just large enough for a bed for their daughter, Eliza.

We loved our nurse, Margie. She had a round, wrinkled, friendly little face. She was a gentle soul, devout, and not unschooled; she religiously completed the crossword puzzle in the *Hartford Times* each evening, wetting the tip of her pencil to press the neat block letters into the refolded pages of the paper. She was generous and devoted to us. One summer night, she won a ten-dollar gold piece at the Catholic Church Fair in Old Saybrook for me and laid it on my pillow for me to discover in the morning. But equally I remember in chagrin how I repaid that generosity of spirit when one day, in a fit of temper, I pounded my fist on her chest. She caught her breath, drew back, and said, "You must never hit a woman there." Since her chest was as flat as any man's, the lesson confused me, but I was ashamed for days.

Under Margie's eyes, we rode our tricycles back and forth along the porch which ran the length of the front of the house. On rainy days in Fenwick, the house was our universe. We overturned the porch furniture, draped chairs and sofas with the rattan porch rugs, and created snug little houses to play in.

Our earliest childhood friends were Hopie and Nancy Bulkeley, grandchildren of the governor by his younger son, Houghton, whom we called Uncle Hought. They were just our ages, Hopie matching my sister Virginia, Nancy matching me. In Hartford, our mothers, living within a street of each other, wheeled their baby carriages together. In Fenwick, we were equally close, a Fenwick block away, and we moved back and forth between the two cottages. In front of their cottage at the road was a stone step for people descending from a carriage. My sister learned to ride a two-wheeler pushing off from this stone.

In Fenwick, it never occurred to me not to play with girls. In my boyhood years in Fenwick, however, boys my age were organized into a play class, which was under the jurisdiction of Twisty, our instructor, mentor, and guide. Where he got his name is obscure to me now, but it could not have come from his attire or appearance. I suppose he was then in his early thirties. His costume consisted of a bow tie, a white shirt, and golfing plus fours. He wore severe-looking rimless glasses. His straight hair was parted in the middle and brushed straight back. Arrayed around him in the inevitable group picture at the end of summer, the eight members of his class were uniformly dressed in khaki shirts and shorts. Twisty led us into a variety of instructive, pleasant, and time-consuming daily activities. Our favorite was building what Twisty named the Cupcake Fleet.

Bachrach

Twisty's Play Class (SWL second from left)

Cupcakes were little bathtubs of boats no more than four feet overall with blunt bows and matching square sterns that we built ourselves in our play class. Working out of Twisty's tool chest, we hammered and sawed in the garage belonging to the family of two members of our group, Bobby and Allen Swain. In Twisty's design, the sides of the boats consisted of one piece of pine board three-eighths of an inch thick. The bottom was tongue and groove planking. The design allowed for six inches of decking fore and aft to keep the water from pouring in.

Propelling a Cupcake was an art in itself. One had to position oneself well forward, keeping crouched in the bow with weight to one side, to hold the boat at an angle. Rather than a paddle, one used a cupped hand for propulsion. By leaning to one side, you could keep the little boat from spinning about aimlessly and steer a reasonably straight course.

All summer, backward and forward, and in sudden spray-making bursts of speed, we paddled furiously about in shallow water, boarding other ships and sinking each other. Bobby Swain was the scourge of the fleet. My spirits sagged when he swooped down on my Cupcake and sank me with one plunging downward thrust of his arm. It was a humiliation often repeated.

When, at the end of summer, the day came for the Cupcake Regatta, Bobby was the clear favorite to win the long-distance race. Twisty lined the boats up at the raft: the Swain brothers, Bobby and Allen; Ed Bulkeley, the son of Morgan Bulkeley; Gray Morrison; the two blond-headed Starrett boys, sons of the builder of the Empire State Building as I was to learn much later; and me, the smallest contestant. The course lay around all the moorings in the harbor, taking us to depths and distances where most of us had never ventured. We waited with hollow stomachs—so many eyes watching from the pier—for the signal to start. In the lineup at the raft, because I was the littlest boatman, I suppose, I was given the pole position. Embarrassed, I saw the others arranged in staggered order behind me. Twisty gave each of us a shove to start us off, beginning with me. For a fraction of a second, I debated whether fairness compelled me to slow down until the others drew abreast, but I decided the situation was too desperate for politeness. I paddled ahead blindly, not daring to look back. I hugged the inside of the course and kept moving expecting Bobby Swain to surge past me at any moment. Miraculously, I held the lead. As I turned the last mooring and headed home, I could see open water between the nearest boat and me. At the railing on the pier, parents and friends cheered us on. They broke into applause as I neared the finish line. No one could have been more astonished than I when I went across in my Cupcake the clear winner. On prize-giving day, I received a medal on a ribbon and applause again.

Chapter 4

Wreck Buoy, Lighthouse, and Home

In Fenwick, in these years, community life was concentrated at the pier, and boating, in larger craft, became the center of life in my boyhood years. The preferred weekend activity was sailboat racing. In later years, Fenwick's large fleet of boats shrank to almost nothing. The reasons for this were many, expense not being chief among them. We had built a good-sized fleet. Through the years, it dwindled. Some of our most dedicated sailors had gone, and we lacked the impetus to start up a new fleet. The focal point of Fenwick life shifted to the golf course. But in those (as I now remember them) carefree days before the Second World War, it was all sailing. There were regular weekend races, one on Saturday afternoon, another on Sunday, after church and after Sunday lunch, which in some houses was often preceded by martini cocktails as a reward for the selfless acts of churchgoing beforehand. Ardent golfers, such as my father, had to fit in their games Saturday morning or Sunday afternoon after the race ended. Many hoped for brisk winds and a fast sail, the quicker to get ashore and onto the golf course. But the serious community interest was all in the sailing.

Almost every family except ours had a boat. Designed by John Alden, they were Indian Class lapstrake centerboard sailboats twenty-one feet in length with mainsail, jib, and spinnaker. There were some twenty boats in all, moored in two lines behind the breakwater just east of the pier since Fenwick had no natural harbor.

In my first term at boarding school, I received a letter from my father. In his neat, schooled hand, he had written across the top of his business letterhead:

Happy Birthday, December 19, 1935
Merry Christmas, December 25, 1935

Below, he wrote that a new Indian Class Fenwick boat (and he gave all the dimensions) was being built for us at a yard in Massachusetts.

The following summer, our boat was delivered from Massachusetts. The gleaming black hull of the already-named *Shadow*, shiny as a patent-leather slipper, was lowered onto the ways of the South Cove. The varnished pine deck flashed in the sun. The *Shadow's* deck with its natural wood finish would become the most distinguishing feature of the new boat when it took its place in the fleet, making her instantly recognizable from the shore.

The boat was worked onto the truck to slide on rails down the ways leading into the shallow cove. The tangle of new rigging was unwound. The rectangular mast was stepped and stayed. Under my apprehensive eye, the new boat was eased into South Cove with scarcely a scratch or scar.

Towed out of the flat cove and into the choppy river, the *Shadow* came around the outer light to the pier. There, Jimmy Willets, who was in charge of the fleet that summer, sat splicing a line on the stern of the committee boat, a double-ended, twenty-eight-foot lifeboat with a cabin and a short mast for a working sail. It was Jimmy's own boat. Jimmy Willets, powerful of build but soft of voice, a gentle giant, was one of my heroes growing up in Fenwick. All of Fenwick was saddened, especially its sailors, when Jimmy, still in his twenties, was electrocuted on a power line working for the Connecticut Light & Power Company. As a funeral tribute, his boat with his ashes was sunk in the Sound.

The *Shadow* was made fast to the pier on the west side just astern of Jimmy's boat. My friend, Gray Morrison, and I tried to puzzle out all the lines. I knew I should have waited until my father got down for the weekend, but I wanted us to be ready to race on Saturday. I was impatient to see the *Shadow* under sail. The new rigging snarled and knotted. The spotless new sails worked stiffly. In time, they would virtually fall into place on mast and boom. Now, the slides stuck. From the stern of his boat, Jimmy looked on with a wise forbearance, only occasionally offering advice. Knowing how long it took to become proficient in boating, he chose not to interfere prematurely.

The breeze was moderate, ideal for a first sail. We cast off—the first mistake. At the tiller, knees trembling, I felt the boat take charge and move. We stood off from the pier. Then, instead of going into the wind gently and coming about, we jibed daringly to return to the pier, and the boom came over hard, accompanied by an alarming ripping sound. The starboard backstay pulled taut, and the track came with it, buckling, drawing the inadequate screws. Substantial bolts were needed instead. The first sail came to an abrupt end. We rounded the pier and headed for our assigned mooring. It was half-tide. Inshore, the sandy bottom came up fast. I could sense the eyes of Jimmy Willets following our errant progress. Our centerboard was up because of the shallow water, and we lost maneuverability, slipping to leeward, losing steerage. Jimmy gave a shout from the pier, and Gray jumped overboard to guide the boat to its mooring. It was a disorderly, humiliating first landing. The halyard was loosened too suddenly. The mainsail came down in a heap, blanketing us both.

In time, I was to learn how to manage that boat properly, becoming in fact a respected skipper in the weekend races. But that was only after many days spent on the water, often entirely alone in my boat, experimenting with the most expeditious ways to handle her in various wind strengths. It meant learning to gauge how far to shoot into the wind without losing momentum completely before going over onto the other tack, and it meant testing the currents and the tides at varying distances from the shore and at different hours in the tide. I learned to spot the back eddies. I noted how closely mainsail and jib should be trimmed going to windward and located the best place to place my weight to balance the tiller.

By taking a position forward beside the centerboard box while sailing alone, at least in a light breeze going to windward, I could handle the boat without touching the tiller—rather like riding a bicycle with no hands—and keep it steady on course simply by shifting my weight forward or backward by an inch or two. Sometimes companionable porpoises would swim alongside, playing about the bow, arching through the water to the rhythm of the boat. The tug of the sail, the wind in one's hair, the water curling off the bow and bubbling astern—there were no other sounds on that whole expanse of water stretching from Fenwick to the far shore. Feeling the boat sail itself pierced the heart and made one want to burst into song.

The race courses were relatively simple and standard weekend after weekend but played differently in different winds and weathers. A usual course was: Wreck Buoy, Lighthouse, and Home, twice around, a simple course and a popular one. It was so familiar that we could sail it in our sleep, but it was still a full test of sailing skill.

The Wreck Buoy, a black-and-red striped can, was positioned about two miles southwest of the pier. It marked a long-forgotten sunken barge. The buoy is no longer there. It was taken away some years ago because it was a nautical redundancy.

Since the prevailing summer winds were southwest, this first leg almost invariably was a beat. One had to tack up the shore inside the worst of the current until one felt sufficiently far west of the buoy to stand out on one tack and make the mark.

Once one turned the buoy, one broke out the spinnaker and ran downwind to the Outer Lighthouse, where the committee boat had placed the next mark. Then it was a short reach back to the pier and the finish line—Home.

Every summer day, I wanted to be nowhere but in my boat. A friend of mine in Fenwick once told me that if his wife hadn't allowed him to have a cruising boat, he would have had to take a mistress. I know what he meant. The boat was an obsession. Life was real on the water. Everything else was illusory.

Shadow

My father was a fresh-breeze sailor. He loved rough going and the salt spray in his face. I was partial to lighter breezes in which subtler racing tactics came into play. I had studied the books and regarded myself as better versed than my father on finer racing points. In a race, I was a nervous, frustrated strategist and occasionally faulted my father on his tactics. He would wear a puzzled look, his partial deafness preventing communication between us.

My sister and I, crewing for him, prided ourselves on how quickly we could break out the spinnaker when we turned the windward mark. The tricky maneuver was usually accompanied by much cursing between us below the level of his hearing, the blame going back and forth if one was slow with the halyard or if the other clumsily fit the spinnaker pole to the mast.

All his life, my father had been deaf in his left ear. His deafness was a problem in our relationship. It distanced me from him, especially when delicate subjects needed to be discussed and the need to speak loudly put a cloak around the subject. If we children really had something on our mind, he would take us for a ride in his car. His hearing was better in his right ear. Seated in the front seat beside him, we could better make ourselves understood.

Yet it was summertime when we were closest to him, when he was away from work and on holiday. We were closest on the water. Critical as I sometimes was, I could not fault my father on his seamanship. His experience came into play one day when he, my brother Ted, who was five years younger than I, and I took the *Shadow* on a day sail across the Sound. We headed for Plum Gut, that narrow rush of water between Orient Point at the tip of the north fork of Long Island and Plum Island, where the old World War I fortifications are now grassed over. On the Connecticut shore, the Plum Island stone lighthouse still flashes the strongest beam.

Coming home, we were caught in the ebbing tide and sent down east. When we were halfway across, the sky darkened. The wind sprang up wildly. The lacing rain of a hard squall dropped like a screen in front of us. With more wind than we could handle, we were knocked nearly flat. My father set about shortening sail by taking in a reef, a procedure that involved bunching the sail and tying in the reef lines. It was a task I had never before undertaken in adverse conditions but had only practiced in the quiet of the harbor at our mooring. My little brother was too small for this work—he was then about ten—and my father and I had to do the job together, as well as keep the boat sailing, going to windward on jib alone so the wind couldn't catch us abeam and knock us over. The footing was slippery, and the boat was riding at a difficult angle. In addition to the rain, we were taking sea water over the rail. In the driving rain on the swinging boom, my father and I managed to put in the necessary reefs and shorten sail. Ted remained in the shelter of the halyard deck, protected and well out of the way of the working crew.

In Fenwick, we were overdue. My distracted and nervous mother, who hated stormy weather and wouldn't herself go near the sea, was in the middle of an afternoon ladies' bridge game at Mrs. Hepburn's and could barely concentrate on the play. She went to the window to search the horizon for our boat but visibility was so limited she could hardly see beyond our harbor breakwater. Two of her children and her husband were out on the sea in the middle of a dangerous storm. Mrs. Hepburn was aware of her concern. Now, the Hepburns, as a family, did not countenance weakness in the face of physical danger in themselves, and it is a family trait to deride it in others.

"Don't worry, Betty," Mrs. Hepburn said with her mischievous smile, as the bridge players put down their hands. "You're young and pretty. You can always get another husband."

We rode out the storm in the middle of the Sound and reached home safely. Abashed as she was at the time by what then seemed only gross insensitivity on the part of a friend, my mother had a keen enough sense of humor to enjoy turning Mrs. Hepburn's remark of that stormy afternoon into an often-told story.

If Jimmy Willets was one hero, Lev Davis was another. They were both some ten to fifteen years older than me. They were thoroughly accomplished in the arts of seamanship, which I sought to learn. So, of course, was my father, and I should have appreciated his sailing skills more at the time. But I favored those of more contemporary and less authoritative models. In the weekend races, Lev, wiry, slight, and deeply tanned, was usually the skipper of the red boat *Nutmeg*, which was always the boat to watch and the boat to beat.

His crew consisted of his older brother, Jack, and his younger brother, Franck Kelso, and sometimes, in place of one of them, his stern-looking father, Colonel Davis, who, far from being the ogre he seemed, became a real friend to me when he was commodore of the Fenwick Yacht Club and I was his chosen secretary-treasurer.

Curiously, in spite of being from a sailing family, Colonel Davis could not swim a stroke. On the pier one day, there was consternation among all those gathered to watch the start of a race when the colonel, smartly clothed in his Sunday outfit—complete with straw hat—jumped recklessly off the pier into the water to fish out his youngest son, Newton, then just three years old, who had unaccountably slipped away from his parents and fallen in. The two non-swimmers were safely brought ashore, but the incident, observed by half of Fenwick, gave us all a scare, not least because it laid bare a weakness in one of the most prominent and respected members of our community.

In our weekend races, usually with Lev and Franck alternating as skippers, the *Nutmeg* had an extraordinary record of success. Many theories and suppositions were advanced to account for this. The real answer was Lev himself; he was incomparably the finest sailor Fenwick ever produced. There was no one to rival him.

In old Fenwick, sailing was the primary activity. Distinction was measured by how many silver goblets you took home for winning a Saturday race. The leading skipper of the summer had his name engraved on the Morgan G. Bulkeley Jr. Memorial Trophy, given in memory of my father's old friend, the elder son of the governor. Our fleet of Indian Class boats had disappeared by the sixties, and even the reduced fleet of lesser Mercuries which succeeded them was dispersed; golf had replaced sailing as the primary activity of the place.

At a high point in the late thirties, the Fenwick fleet numbered some twenty boats. Several owners were not Fenwick-based but came from upriver, like Bill Burt in his yellow *Canary*. Bill's family had a house on the river with a dock on Lord Cove just above the highway bridge. Moored midstream was their forty-seven-foot Alden-designed cutter *Halcyone* on which I was sometimes invited to sail. Tied up at the dock was a Chris-Craft speedboat that Bill would use to commute downriver for the races.

Further up the cove, the Burts also owned another fine old river house, Tannemahaig, with a commanding downriver view of the Sound. Over the summers, it had several distinguished tenants. One summer, it was Albert Einstein; another summer, President James Bryant Conant of Harvard stayed there. I think these great men must have loved their ruddy, plain-spoken landlord, Chicago-born William G. Burt, a retired executive of Sears, Roebuck and Company, who delighted in taking them sailing aboard his fine boat. Going through Plum Gut on *Halcyone* one afternoon with Conant aboard, we passed a barge with a small barking terrier protesting our presence from its stern deck. I watched in surprise as the president of Harvard barked back.

But in all those years before the war, there was no sight to equal that of Bill Burt sweeping past our Fenwick pier in his speedboat with Einstein in the forward seat next to him, his wild, white hair flying. The boat did not stop. It made one curving pass off the end of the pier and then headed out into the Sound. But those of us standing on the pier that day had the image stamped forever in our memories of the unmistakable figure of Albert Einstein giddily in motion over the water, his face sunny with childlike pleasure.

Lev, notwithstanding, the most prominent sailor in our weekend races was Houghton Bulkeley, skipper of *Lady Fenwick*. The younger brother of my father's good friend, Uncle Hought was much loved. The scowling look and heavy jowls disguised a softer nature. I see him digging in the earth around his scraggly hedge or at our bulkhead where he would take his noontime swim, wearing his blue swimming shorts below his high protruding stomach and a white towel across his shoulders while he chatted gallantly with the lady swimmers. On the golf course, I see him taking his quick, foreshortened swing. I remember his sharp-eyed inspection trips around the borough made as warden of Fenwick (our mayor) in his golf cart. I can also see him in a rear pew in the chapel on Sunday, the only day in the week when he would climb out of his worn dungarees to put on white trousers and a blue Fenwick blazer.

He was kind to us as children and would become a warm friend to my wife later. He was noted for his fairness as warden and was universally respected. And yet, on the water, to those watching from other boats as he sat hunched in the cockpit of *Lady Fenwick*, his tiller crooked under his arm, his visored hat framing a glowering look, he was a formidable, even fearsome rival. He was strict about the rules of racing. Across the years, I still hear his bellowed shout of "Buoy room!" when he held the inside position at a mark. Buoy Room Bulkeley—he was not reluctant to register a protest after the race if he felt he had been wronged on the course. In argument on land, I can see the firm, quick shake of his head, shaking the loose jowls, as he defended his claim and denied the offending person's defense.

Uncle Hought was human and could be wrong. There was, for instance, that ludicrous accident one year in a Labor Day race when he tipped over ignominiously in the *Lady Fenwick* in the river. The race came after the golf tournament when the Morgan Cup was filled with gin and passed among "former winners." As a former winner, Uncle Hought had claimed his turn at the cup.

The course that day took us into the river where a northwest breeze sprang up sending strong puffs of wind across the flattened water. Uncle Hought must have cleated his main sheet. A gust of wind caught him flat-footed and knocked him over. There he was, Uncle Hought, in his bulky blue sailing jersey, with his red visored hat pulled low across his eyes, the tiller hugged under his arm, sinking incomprehensibly into the river. For years, we laughed over that Labor Day race, Uncle Hought right along with us.

Chapter 5

Nineteen Thirties

Growing up in Fenwick in the 1930s, at my age, I was not especially aware of the Great Depression. It was not spoken of so far as I can remember, at least not in my hearing, possibly because in strict New England after years of post-World-War-I prosperity, it would have been an indecency to mention it. In the manufacturing world of Hartford to which my father belonged and in the insurance world in which he was also inevitably involved, the Depression obviously was not without serious consequences. Yet, I was never aware of any personal hardship endured by my family or their friends. Certainly, life in Fenwick went on as before.

Two years before the crash, my father had sold our house on North Beacon Street in Hartford, exchanging it for a finer new stucco dwelling with entrances on two levels and a porte-cochere covering the lower one. It stood at the very peak of the high hill of Prospect Avenue, overlooking the whole city. Its steep backyard descended in terraces to a small orchard of apple trees below in a wild patch of ground we entered only on our most adventuresome days. We had a whole new world to explore from a small backyard at North Beacon Street. We were proud of our new home, as surely our father was too, even if it was an effort to pump our bicycles up Prospect Hill to the very top. We passed the houses of many of Hartford's wealthiest citizens on the way. Living on top of the finest hill in Hartford inclined one to totally unfounded delusions of superiority.

If my father experienced strain in maintaining in addition to the Fenwick place this fine new property located among such magnificent company on the city's premier residential street, he never let on.

Socially, leaving the exceptional Hepburns aside, Fenwick in the 1930s consisted of two circles of different ages and ways of entertaining. They did not intersect. Below the sedate circle my father and mother belonged to was another livelier, sometimes rowdy one, post-Prohibition in behavior and attitude. My father's golfing companions were the businessmen of Hartford, all high officers of important Hartford enterprises. There was no mixing of wives in their games. Vaguely avuncular in relation to us children, these prominent men inspired respect. With the men dressed in coats and ties and women in light summer dresses, my parents' group gave dinner parties, played bridge, and were early to bed. They ruled Fenwick in monarchial self-assurance while the younger set partook of giddier pleasures. If our parents had a dinner party and the guests were assembled in the living room, my sister and I would steal out of bed, creep halfway down the staircase, crouch below the banister rail, and spy on the guests through a hole in the wall of the banister.

My sister remembers our father and mother in an earlier day dressed in formal clothes, my mother in a long evening dress and my father in a dinner jacket, walking down the seafront to have dinner with Nana Bulkeley, widow of Governor Bulkeley. She inevitably served lobster, which our father did not eat, but she always provided something else for him.

Eight to ten years younger and in very different costumes, the other circle gathered in the late thirties for Saturday night picnics behind the Keeneys' garage, a field away from our cottage, or on the beach around a bonfire. The parties were convivial and bibulous and grew noisy as the long summer evening progressed. This group was my mother's age, but she never attended their picnics. There was never any question of her doing anything but following her husband and taking her place in the older group, her natural high spirits subordinated to their more seemly behavior.

In our pre-teen years, we boys in the twilight hours after supper and into the evening marauded about Fenwick on our bicycles under the brazen banner of the Poison Patrol. Bobby Swain was the brash leader of our escapades. His nervy younger brother, Allen, tagged along behind, struggling like the rest of us to keep up. Bobby was bigger and stronger than any of us and unchallenged as the best athlete. He led us to commit one of our worst misdeeds one evening by tying up one younger sister to a lamppost and leaving her helpless but tearless for half an hour. We had to salute her bravery.

It was Bobby who challenged me to a coal-throwing contest one day behind the red garage of the Swain's cottage. Each cottage had coal bins in those days to feed the stoves, but only Bobby thought to appropriate coal as ammunition. We stood about ten yards apart, each armed with an ashcan cover as a shield, and started hurling. I had to return home that day and explain to my mother why I had a chipped front tooth, which had resulted from a slip in my defenses.

Cut off as it was from the main roads and town traffic, all of Fenwick was open to us—its roads and yards and paths, the broad fairways of its golf course, and the long front sidewalk past all the first-row cottages, with its line of globe-lit lampposts running down to the pier. The bathhouse at the pier, that magnetic playground of our youth, did not survive the 1938 hurricane. It was a last remaining legacy of Edward Stokes' sojourn in Fenwick.

It was to these pre-1938 hurricane years that I date my awareness of Katharine Hepburn. I remember seeing her very early in her career on the stage of the Ivoryton Theater, that fine old summer stock theater. It must have been Fenwick night. The play was *The Cat and the Canary*. Ivoryton was surely happy to provide some early experience to a promising local girl, incidentally gaining lasting retroactive fame thereby. My recollection of the play is dim, although my memory of seeing someone from Fenwick on the stage—an actress in our midst—is brighter. Later, I would encounter her close up on the porch of the Hepburn's cottage.

Mrs. Hepburn had established a family custom of serving tea on the porch every afternoon at five o'clock, and anyone was welcome to come. Mrs. Hepburn passed on to her children her good looks, the doctor his robust physical exuberance. She was frankly pleased with their good looks, he with their athleticism. She counted it one of life's pleasures to have good-looking children. She would say so, and you would somehow be embraced, too, in the self-flattery. Usually several Hepburn children decorated these teas. When I was old enough, I started going. Occasionally, Kate would be there. It was then that my unreasoning worship of Kate Hepburn began.

It was a challenge to go to those open-house teas Mrs. Hepburn presided over on the porch every afternoon. Along with the outspoken Hepburn children, a famous guest from the outside world of theater, film, medicine, or politics was often present. I felt disloyal to my own family for sometimes attending those teas and receiving indoctrination from Mrs. Hepburn in the brand of Fabian Socialism the Hepburns espoused. It was not the Hartford way.

"Come, Stuie, sit by me," she would say. "Tell me what you've been doing. What have you been reading?" She once urged me to read a book containing the Soviet constitution that she praised as a remarkably sensible document. In every other cottage on the beach, including our own, her ideas, of course, were anathemas. In disapproving of the Hepburns, my mother was inclined to characterize them simply as eccentric. To a New Englander, that was a sufficiently damning adjective. The Hepburns' self-reliance in the face of disapproval cast a light on our own inadequacies and dependencies, their spirit of adventure on our timidity.

At those teas, Mrs. Hepburn was very much the central figure, surrounded by her high-spirited and opinionated children. The more outrageous in argument they were, the more she was amused, and she never chided or corrected them. Mrs. Hepburn led the discussion to elicit responses from her sometimes mortified guests. She was a strong, handsome woman, her sharp cheekbones reflected, perhaps accentuated, in Kate. She was a shameless flatterer, but as recipient of her compliments, one was all too willing to read her attention as encouragement and her encouragement as approval and praise.

Already well known, Kate was a dazzling presence on those occasions when she returned home from her unknown world, which was impossible for us to imagine, and assumed a place on the porch as just another member of the family. From her father, the doctor, she took her reddish complexion, her robust love of sport, and her fearlessness. He would quote to her from the prefaces of Shaw, the reigning playwright in the Hepburn household.

Later, more worshipful than ever, I would see Kate Hepburn in a variety of circumstances, business-related and otherwise—interviewing her backstage at the Shubert Theater in New Haven for the *Yale Daily News* after she performed in a Philip Barry play *Without Love;* at a rehearsal at the American Shakespeare Festival in Stratford, Connecticut, when she was playing Cleopatra; when she came to our cottage on an impromptu visit; playing tennis with her on the Fenwick courts; and spending time with her on the set of her last film *Grace Quigley.*

And then there was our canoe trip the summer of 1938. She and Howard Hughes had come in from a long sail and were moored. I had been out in *Shadow,* had unrigged the boat, and was cleaning up. That summer, Hughes visited Kate several times, sometimes arriving by seaplane to the enchantment of Fenwick's boys and girls. The newspapers were avidly following the Hepburn-Hughes romance. They spent time together on the golf course—they were both excellent golfers—and once, to our excitement, my father, who was among the best golfers in Fenwick, was invited to play with them. Since both my father and Hughes were deaf, I have often wondered how that game went.

By now, it was late afternoon. The sky had clouded over in the southwest, and the wind was picking up, causing some chop at the entrance to our little harbor. Tied up at their mooring fifty yards from mine, Kate and Hughes lowered sail. I was about ready to go ashore myself when I heard Kate announcing in a loud voice, "Never mind, Howard, I'll swim ashore and get a boat." I noticed for the first time that they had no tender astern.

To the exclusion of everything else, I was conscious of the presence of these two famous people only fifty yards away. I was in awe of Kate, a helpless admirer from afar. Now I had a chance to become a hero in her sight. Summoning my courage, I called over offering to pick them up and take them ashore. I had our canoe tied astern. It was one of my father's conceits to have a canoe instead of a dinghy as a tender for our boat.

Even in the protected zone behind the breakwater, it was getting rough. I loaded my sail bag into the canoe and pushed off for the Hepburns' boat. In a moment, I had the canoe alongside. Kate tossed their sail bag aboard, and Hughes got into the bow. Normally, my father would supervise the careful disposition of weight so that the canoe was in good balance, but I couldn't order about Hepburn and Hughes. Kate enjoyed any little adventure. She got in amidships and faced me. Her hair was held in a bandana tied beneath her chin and she wore her familiar white trousers. Her smile came straight out of a movie screen. I put my mind to paddling. The one thing I could not do was capsize with these passengers aboard.

Bow-heavy, we set out for the pier. The waves heaped up in the open water between the breakwater and the end of the pier. Somehow, I had to navigate that opening to bring the canoe safely alongside the landing raft.

Kate talked to me the whole time.

"You love sailing, don't you?" (*She knew I was a sailor!*)

"I often see you in your boat." (*She had seen me!*)

"Did you have a good sail today? Where did you go?" (*We had been comrades at sea!*)

Concentrating on my paddling, eyeing the waves rolling in, I could hardly form any sensible answer. Hughes, throughout, never uttered a word.

On the pier, people stood waiting for us to come in. Kate's romance with Hughes during that summer of 1938 was a topic of national interest. Newspaper speculation over whether they would marry was at white heat. I was more aware of Hughes' reputation as a flyer. In January of 1937, he had broken the transcontinental flight record, spanning the country in seven and a half hours. His next challenge was to circle the globe, a flight that would take him over Nazi Germany against the objections of Hitler and on across the Siberian range. He was by then as famous as Kate, matching her in audacity, accomplishment, and extravagant behavior.

With heavy waves rolling in, the crests and troughs became deeper due to the shallowing water in the falling tide, and I had to keep the bow into the wind and slide crabwise toward the pier. Hughes took the spray in his face, but I couldn't worry about that. And Kate, facing me half kneeling in the canoe, kept talking. There was no chance to dwell on the story I could bring to the dinner table that night, and it wasn't over yet.

We eased our way toward the pier. At last, we made it, coming in broadside to the raft, which at this tide, floated nearly six feet below the level of the pier. I congratulated myself. I was relieved to have brought off the rescue. Above, along the rail, a line of people waited to see the famous couple come ashore. Kate tossed the sail bags up on the raft. Expectantly, I awaited a smile of thanks, if not from the dour, uncommunicative Hughes, at least from my heroine, Kate. It was not to be. Just then, a man on the pier lowered a newspaper, exposing the lens of a news camera, and snapped a picture of Katharine Hepburn and Howard Hughes in the canoe. Kate was on her feet instantly.

"God damn it, Howard," she snapped. "Go get him!"

Hughes, seated in the canoe, made no move. A disgusted Kate hopped onto the raft, bounded up the rock staircase to the top of the pier, and gave chase. At the end of the pier, a hundred yards away, the photographer had parked his car. He reached the car, clutching his camera, and made good his escape. By that time, Hughes had clambered ashore with the sail bag, and I was left alone with the canoe.

On my own internal movieola, I have played and replayed this scene many times. Each time, it ends with Kate angrily running off without a parting smile for me—that brilliant Hepburn smile. I was left with the image of something else instead—that of her private and fiercely independent self.

It was in the following year that Kate came out of the career slump that earned her the insulting epithet of "box office poison." She scored her enormous stage success in *The Philadelphia Story* and by accepting

Howard Hughes' advice to sew up the film rights for herself, secured her financial future as well.

That fall, the hurricane of 1938 in effect remade the map of Fenwick. The Hepburn cottage beyond the pier was completely demolished. A Hepburn family film shows Kate in the aftermath mugging in the debris, sitting defiantly in a bathtub marooned in a sea of sand as if to say no storm was so great as to drown her spirits. In fact, the Hepburns hardly lost a beat in building a new house on the same site, a rambling, white-painted brick colonial house with rooms for all the Hepburns plus visitors and sturdy enough to withstand any storm. It was up by the following summer. Next door to the Hepburns, on low ground behind the pier, the Morgan B. Brainard cottage was washed away by the waters of the storm.

The Cottage before the Hurricane of '38

Next in severity of damage further up the beach was our cottage. I was in school in Massachusetts at the time of the storm. Coming in from afternoon sports with friends, I watched appalled as the earth heaved up around the base of a large oak tree directly in our path, exposing the roots. The old tree tipped and fell to the ground.

The surviving post-hurricane photograph of our cottage in Fenwick showed the damage so vividly as to lead me to think I had actually been there to take the blows. All the porches—on the west, on the south, and on the east—were stripped away, leaving the shell of the house standing, bare in many places of its shingles, sitting in a heap of sand and stones thrown up on our front lawn by the force of the waves.

The Morning After

After that storm, my father's insurance agent called to inquire why my father had not made a claim on his hurricane insurance policy. My father had forgotten ever buying such a policy. Living in the insurance capital of

Hartford and being a director of Aetna Life, he believed implicitly in insurance and had loaded himself with policies. It skipped his mind that a hurricane policy on the house in Fenwick was among them. Whatever the circumstances, there was absolutely no question but that he would restore the cottage at least to its former condition, but the insurance certainly helped.

In the following years, Fenwick was to be visited by more hurricanes—Carol in 1954, Diane in 1955, Donna in 1960, Gloria in 1985—but none of them, feared as they were on arrival, matched the 1938 hurricane in destructiveness. Thirty-eight, however, taught us to be wary and instructed us in the vulnerability especially of the shorefront cottages. Surely, it was a factor in my eventual decision to sell. Unlike my father, if another killer hurricane came, I was treading such a fine line financially in keeping up the place from year to year, with annual maintenance costs peculiar to seaside property, that I could not have managed any extraordinary expense resulting from heavy storm damage on top of everything else. After 1938, no such thing as affordable private hurricane insurance existed anymore; there was only government insurance.

Chapter 6

Greener Fields

From the causeway, we looked across the broad mouth of the Connecticut River to Old Lyme. The late afternoon sun lit the Lyme shore and brightened the slim white steeple of the Congregational church, which was almost lost in the greenery of the trees. High on the hills overlooking river and Sound, one or two large houses could be made out shining in the sun, and one wondered now at the life that went on in those great, protected, enclosed estates. Old Lyme seemed very rich to us. Old Lyme, furthermore, had a country club, unlike Fenwick, and Saturday night dances.

Free and forgiving as was Fenwick, in our mid-teens, we searched for new territory beyond the boundaries of the borough. (Was Fenwick really all that good? we wondered.) The opportunity to receive a driver's license at the age of sixteen opened up a whole world of new girls and new companions across the river in Lyme. The Lyme dances drew us out of Fenwick. The trip across the river brought with it a loss of innocence—a new, unsettling dissatisfaction with what we had always known, guilty knowledge of the limitations of what our parents had given us.

Were the girls prettier in Lyme? Yes, we decided. At a beach picnic one Saturday night, I noticed a blonde girl with incongruously dark, defined eyebrows, wearing white shorts. She was bewitching. Instantly, I was in love. Since she was in the company of equally admiring boys from her side of the river, at such a time, at such an age, I couldn't really do anything about it. I sat there and admired this new sight, momentarily exhilarated by the realization that I, as a newcomer, had awakened an interest in her, such that for some blissful moments and for several Saturdays in a row that summer, she and I became an expected pair. All of life was not in Fenwick.

In July of 1939, when my friend and next-door neighbor Gray Morrison and I were seventeen, in our second summer with driver's licenses, Madge Evans was starring in a summer stock production of *Biography* at the Ivoryton Playhouse. As did many Ivoryton players in those days, Miss Evans, during her run, was staying in Fenwick at the Riversea Inn. The inn was managed as a kind of summer adjunct of the Adirondacks Club, a similar sort of resort hotel appealing to the same sort of clientele. Its guests consisted partly of Hartford widows who had friends or relatives in Fenwick. They walked down the tar road from the inn to the pier in light, flowery print dresses with frilly collars that seemed more appropriate to city garden parties than to Fenwick strolls. And then, jarringly, there was the occasional star of an Ivoryton production with bright makeup and penciled eyebrows.

Watching her movies and pictures, Gray and I became enamored of Madge Evans. We made a plan to take a trip to Ivoryton to see her in *Biography*. If we got up the nerve, we decided, we would send her a note backstage at intermission offering to drive her home to Fenwick and return her to the Riversea Inn. All went as planned, and she met us smiling backstage after the performance. Still wearing her stage makeup, she was heart-stoppingly pretty. We couldn't believe our good fortune—Madge Evans in the front seat of the car sitting between the two sophisticates.

En route home, we stopped at Dutchland Farms for ice cream sodas, just like a date, and she kept up a merry chatter about our lives in Fenwick and inquired about our interest in theater. Our interest was for the moment very much star-driven.

At last, the time came to take her back to the inn. There was a flurry at the door as we arrived. The desk clerk breathlessly informed Miss Evans that a telegram had arrived for her. She rushed in to receive it, curtailing our goodnights. We did not see her again. The next week, she moved on with *Biography* to Ogunquit, Maine. Later, in the papers, we were crushed to read that while there, she and Sidney Kingsley, the playwright, were married. We had lost her so quickly.

The fantasy love gave way to a real one, and reality, one would learn, had its drawbacks. But they were not to be thought of in those soft summer nights with Penny. She was fifteen when I met her. She had long, golden hair, which was untrained and somewhat frizzy, a high rounded brow, and a fetching mole high on her left cheek. When expressing puzzlement or dismay, she had a habit of stroking her chin. The gesture expressed embarrassment or was meant to convey helplessness, as in "I'd like things to be different, but, as you see, I can't really do anything about it." Once, I saw her being driven away to New London to take the ferry to Fishers Island. She was on her way to stay with her father who was divorced from her mother. My foresighted rival in love at the time anticipated her need before I did and won the right to drive her to New London. As they drove out of Fenwick, she saw me in the road looking wanly after them, and she stroked her chin out the window as, I thought, a signal that she would have preferred her driver to be me.

Penny lived with her mother in a farmhouse just outside of Fenwick that they rented for the summer. They would come to Fenwick to swim. New Yorkers transplanted from Pennsylvania, they were Quakers, thee-thou-ing each other out of the presence of strangers. Both of them were by nature artistic—the mother being a sculptor, Penny already gifted as a writer. With a strong streak of what was then called bohemianism, they were foreigners to Fenwick, in sharp contrast to my other companions and the interrelated Hartford families. On weekends, Penelope's mother entertained a male friend who was the editor of an important New York literary publication. When the following year I was in college working for the undergraduate newspaper, he said to me in a kindly, fraternal fashion, "The difference between us is that I work for a weekly and you work for a daily." For some reason, I was at the time deeply flattered by the collegial act of his calling attention to this distinction.

After our first summer, throughout the years she spent in boarding school in Holmquist, New Jersey, we wrote each other letters. She wrote so spontaneously, so fluidly, with such feeling and style, responding so openly to everything she read and studied, that I kept the letters for years.

Literary enthusiasms were partly the basis for my relationship with Penelope, although I sensed in her, along with stirrings in myself, a passionate nature. Our goodnights in the car outside the farmhouse were sweet and protracted, never interrupted by her mother, although once when my mother suggested that we together might have been exposed to some running summer disease, Penny's mother, protective of her fifteen-year-old daughter, said, "There are some things worse than that."

I gave her no cause to worry about the boundaries of our relationship. Once, as I was driving in a car, as Penny was sitting close, I felt through my arm the outline of her breast under her light summer blouse, and neither she nor I pulled away. Our goodnight kisses were long and passionate. Our relationship, more realistically, was colored by our mutual involvement during those summers in such literary enthusiasms as the novels of Virginia Woolf and the poems of Matthew Arnold. *To the Lighthouse* was our favorite text, and we had our own lighthouse beckoning at the end of its long breakwater reaching out into the Sound. Arnold's "Dover Beach" was our poem, his mournful sentiments suiting the temper of our summertime infatuation, played against the distant rumble of war in Europe.

> Ah, love, let us be true
> To one another! for the world, which seems
> To lie before us like a land of dreams,
> So various, so beautiful, so new,
> Hath really neither joy, nor love, nor light,
> Nor certitude, nor peace, nor help for pain;
> And we are here as on a darkling plain
> Swept with confused alarms of struggle and flight,
> Where ignorant armies clash by night.

Still, summer stretched longingly towards the infinite future; we would be together always.

Our life together was not all mooning in a car. Our last summer was spent working on a summer weekly called *Connecticut Shore*. The paper covered summer resorts from Madison to the west of Fenwick to Black Point on the east. We were hired together by the editor and instigator of the paper, Mary Palmer, who was also blonde and beautiful, in fact, almost certainly an image of what Penny might one day become, and our senior by perhaps eight years. Mary was an experienced journalist, having already put in time at *Newsweek*. She was later to become London correspondent for that magazine during the war. She had a whimsical talent, too, for cartooning. Her little drawings appeared weekly. We were the paper's main reporters. She pointed us to weekly features which we researched and wrote jointly, interviewing one week a famous poet who lived in Lyme, another week a retired tugboat captain and river pilot who lived in a cottage on Saybrook Point which we passed going into Fenwick. In that article, we noted how, in a fit of bashfulness, our captain kept rolling his cap around his head. Our faces burned when he made it clear to us afterwards that he didn't like our reference, and so we learned early of the embarrassments that can come from overly personal reporting.

On one memorable assignment, Penny and I went backstage at the Ivoryton Playhouse after a matinee performance of Eugene O'Neill's *The Emperor Jones* to interview Paul Robeson. Famous as he was, Robeson was welcoming and kindly to the young, green journalists. He was not a bit condescending as he described his efforts to learn African dialects and languages so that he could become better acquainted with his land of origin and his learning Russian to communicate more freely with a people to whom he felt kinship. Robeson's wife Eslanda came along to his dressing room. In his rich baritone, he sang out the tune he used to summon her, and the interview was over, but not before he had given us ample time and his full attention. We went away convinced that we had scored a journalistic triumph.

Putting the paper together, we worked in idyllic circumstances in a one-room cabin in the woods in Old Lyme. Mary made the work fun, and at the end of the week, we collected the articles, the columns, the artwork, and the ad copy and headed down Route 1 to Stonington to deliver everything to the printer. There and in college, these early attempts in journalism directed me to what in later life was to become my main professional work.

Penny and I saw each other constantly and did everything together. We lived in a strange kind of innocence. One evening, at the end of the summer, we went down to Ocean Beach, the amusement park outside New London. On the spur of the moment, we decided to go swimming in the park pool among the foreign New Londoners. We rented bathing suits and changed in the bathhouse. Penny appeared in a plain black knitted one-piece suit. She was embarrassed. There was a moth hole in the seat of her suit. We knew each other well enough to overcome any embarrassment. She pointed to it and giggled. We dove in and played together in the pool like children, roughhousing in the water as perhaps we would not have done in Fenwick. Our arms touched, our legs touched in the lighted pool. We lunged at each other and darted away. It was one of our last evenings of that summer. She would be going off to college, and I would be returning to Yale. But we promised to see each other again in September, when she would come up to Hartford and visit for my sister's engagement party.

On that visit, in the evening, we took a long emotional drive into the country, unhappy over our impending separation but certain that our love was lasting. We parked by the side of the road, darkness all around us. In our embrace her hand brushed along my trousers, not accidentally, and the moment came and passed when we might, that once, have forsworn our innocence and made real love, the culmination of all our summer nights. After that visit, we were to see each other only once more.

The thirties had come to an end, and my view of Fenwick was changing as war approached. It seemed smaller and farther away. I was now in my sophomore year at Yale and Penny in her first year at Swarthmore. In our changed circumstances, our view of each other altered. The fall of that sophomore year had been full, but I arranged a weekend in early December to visit Penny in college. I sensed that our relationship had changed, and I suspected what the trouble was. Coming from all-male Yale, I had been apprehensive that in co-educational Swarthmore, she would have attracted new intellectual companions with whom I could not compete. Throughout the weekend, she was correct in all ways, showing me the campus, the library, the theater, introducing me to favorite professors, taking me to the Saturday night dance. But she was distant and reserved. We did not kiss. At no time during the weekend did I encounter "him," and neither of us raised the subject, but of the existence of someone new in her life, I was certain. Miserable in the knowledge that our relationship of two years was now over and that a carefree period in my life had come to an end, I headed back to New Haven by train. It was December 7, 1941. On the train, I learned of the bombing of Pearl Harbor.

When I reached New Haven, I reported at once to the *Yale Daily News* where I had been a staff member since early in freshman year. The Monday front page was being reworked feverishly. But something was missing—a statement from President Seymour, who was bedridden with a cold in the president's house on Hillside Avenue.

With my good friend Jim Buckley, I stood in the heeler's room of the *News* building. We hit upon an idea. We would stir up a response by fabricating a demonstration. Joined by our good friend, Seth Taft, we started in the courtyard of Vanderbilt Hall at the south end of the Old Campus and began banging garbage can covers to attract attention. The courtyard soon filled with Vanderbilt freshmen. The beginning of a procession formed behind us.

We led the march north on College Street in the direction of the president's house on Hillside Avenue. Shouting and cheering, now many hundreds strong, we marched to the president's house and called for his appearance. President Seymour, the tall, distinguished historian of Versailles with his polished bald head and elegant manners, appeared. In measured words, he urged on us moderation, discipline, and steadfastness.

With his brief remarks, Jim, Seth, and I had our story: a statement from the president. We returned hurriedly to the *News* Building leaving the marchers to go their own way. The Monday front page was remade. By midnight, Buckley, Taft, and I were in a car on our way to Washington for the declaration of war.

The Taft cousins of Ohio, Lloyd and Seth, were classmates and friends. Grandsons of a president of the United States, they were the fourth generation of Tafts to enter Yale. Lloyd, sandy-haired, argumentative, brilliant, and sometimes unpredictable, was especially prominent as the son of Senator Robert A. Taft. In the family tradition, Lloyd was to emerge as a formidable debater in the Yale Political Union. Seth was the son of the senator's popular younger brother, Charles P. Taft. Lanky and curly-haired, he was conscientious, scholarly, and the most systematically well-prepared student I knew, with the possible exception of my roommate John B. Goodenough, who was to end up the number one student in our class with the inevitable commencement-time joke about his name. Seth was more predictable than his cousin and less social and outgoing but became president of the Yale Political Union as well as vice chairman, later acting chairman, of the *News*.

For the moment, we were all simply sophomores driving through the night to be present in the capital when war was declared. Jim and I rode with Seth in one car, Lloyd and Bob Sweet (later to become a district court judge in New York) in another. The all-night drive brought us red-eyed into Washington in time for an early breakfast. I recall being moved by the symbolism of the first stop we made on that sunny but deeply shadowed morning in Washington. We drove directly to the home of the widow of President Taft. Seth disappeared into the house to pay his respects to his grandmother.

After that stop, we continued to the Senate office building. Jim would one day have an office in this building as a United States senator from New York, and go on to have a remarkable career in government: high office in the State Department, head of Radio Free Europe/Radio Liberty, and service on the second highest court in the land as judge of the United States Court of Appeals in Washington.

Senator Taft, bald and severe-looking behind his rimless glasses, set out at a brisk walk, the five of us following, and told us in a few businesslike words what to expect. At noon, Congress would convene in a joint session.

The members of the Cabinet and the justices of the Supreme Court would take their places on the House floor. The president would enter at 12:30. After his address, which was expected to be short and to recommend a declaration of war, the Senate and the House would convene separately to take their votes.

We joined Martha Taft, the senator's plump, pleasant wife, in the lounge reserved for the wives of senators. The tall, draped windows looked out on the Capitol grounds. Over the loudspeakers, we heard the words of a prayer in the hushed House chamber and then the familiar accent of the president as he began: "Yesterday, December 7, 1941—a date that will live in infamy—the United States of America was suddenly and deliberately attacked by naval and air forces of the empire of Japan …"

By the accident of college friendships and through our connection with the *Yale Daily News*, Jim Buckley and I had been at the center when these historic words were spoken. As we drove back to New Haven, it seemed to us that our roles in this war had already commenced. Some members of our class enlisted at once, and our first war casualty came only nine months after Pearl Harbor. For most of us, the delay before we put on the uniform was more protracted, and college went on.

Fenwick now seemed distant. Images of Penny were no longer in my head. My boat, my friends, our cottage, and even my family had receded into the past.

Chapter 7

Hartford and Hepburn

The bloodlines of Hartford ran strong in Fenwick. And in spite of out-of-state transfusions in recent years, they remain strong today. Bulkeleys, Brainards, Goodwins, and Davises, whose forebears were among the founders, are still prominent in Fenwick. Their names are engraved on its treasured athletic trophies over and over again.

As strongly as Hartford has left its mark, so has Hartford's then-dominant commercial enterprise, the Aetna Life Insurance Company. No fewer than three of Aetna's chief executives have lived in Fenwick: Governor Bulkeley, Morgan Bulkeley Brainard, and Olcott D. Smith. Governor Bulkeley was succeeded by his nephew, Brainard. As Ellsworth S. Grant reports in his *A Connecticut Journey*, a newspaper reporter, inquiring about the succession, asked Brainard to what did he attribute his rise to the office. Brainard replied, "Why, of course to my sterling character and worth." When he saw the reporter copying down his words, Brainard laughed and said, "Don't write that. You better say I became president because my uncle was president before me."

Upon his death, Morgan Brainard's Fenwick house was bought by Lucy Brainerd Smith, Brainard's niece, and her husband, Olcott. Out of the same house, then, came the next Aetna president, Olcott Smith, whose father coincidentally was Aetna's chief counsel and Brainard's best friend—Fenwick all the way.

At one period of Fenwick's history, in the 1940s and 1950s, four of Aetna's top executives, including a director or two, of whom my father was one, owned cottages in Fenwick. In an afternoon on the Fenwick golf course, Aetna policy could have been set and coordinated within a single foursome. Aetna was so pervasive an influence in Fenwick that it was a shock one day to hear that the mother of our next-door neighbor had willed her daughter stock in the Traveler's Insurance Company, Aetna's arch rival. And, as her jubilant husband boasted, it was in a single certificate with a value of one million dollars.

The strong business ethos implanted by Hartford in Fenwick had an antidote in the Hepburn family. They were outnumbered in Fenwick but not outmatched. While they had settled in Hartford and their loyalties were to Hartford, the doctor was a Virginian by birth and Mrs. Hepburn was related to the Houghtons of Corning, New York. In those years, practically everyone else in Fenwick was Connecticut-born. To me, young as I was, the Hepburns and their way of life were exciting and attractive. Hartford people brought just Hartford people to Fenwick: predictable ideas, predictable politics. One could not be sure where the Hepburns' friends came from. Their house hummed with unexpected happenings. Through their actress daughter and through their friends and associations, they were connected to the outside world. I was curious—curious but conflicted, drawn to them but at the same time distanced from them, not remotely part of their world at all.

The Hepburns, as I have said, were of Fenwick and yet at the same time apart from Fenwick. I had a number of talks with Kate that touched on this point when she was making her last film, *Grace Quigley*, in and around New York. With her cooperation and that of her director and great friend Anthony Harvey, I hoped to write a book about Fenwick's most famous inhabitant, bringing together the actress at work with the Kate who throughout her life regarded this place as her true home.

"They were courageous people," Kate said about her parents one day during one of our meetings on the set. "After all, they stood for things the community didn't want any part of—my father fighting against venereal disease and prostitution, two subjects you didn't mention, and my mother for the women's vote and birth control. It affected me, knowing the community disapproved, when I was a kid. I knew I wasn't part of the club. I think it was what made me want to be an actor. I wanted to get out of there."

In her young years, Kate rebelled, not against her family but against the community for disapproving of her family.

When she talked to you, Kate Hepburn gave you her whole attention, and nothing she said was rehearsed or in any way canned. She was talking to you, and it was always new, thought out, and freshly felt.

I remember the day one summer Kate asked if she could come over to our house to wash her hair, which was a daily ritual for her. The boiler in her house had gone out, and there was no hot water.

She arrived by bike, bearing, as I remember, a section of a freshly baked cake. We showed her into the kitchen and introduced her to the pantry sink, which was entirely to her liking.

When she had finished and emerged with a towel wrapped around her head, we walked out to the front yard where we stood chatting. She completely surprised me with her memories. Somehow, her film-star fame, which usually caused such awe and speechlessness in me, disappeared, and she became just a Fenwick neighbor. She glanced around her—she had not been up at our end of the beach for a while—and spotted the relatively new swimming pool that three neighbors had built in an adjoining lot.

"They've done that all wrong," Kate declared. "I come from the land of swimming pools and, believe me, that high fence just cuts out all the air. You'd swelter in there."

She herself was a Sound swimmer exclusively. "Anyway, I say better the dirt you don't know than the dirt you do."

Kate then turned to me speaking seriously. "You know when we were living in Hawthorne Street in Hartford and your grandmother lived right across the street, I can remember your father courting your mother. He'd come to the house in his car to pay a visit."

Kate had a strong sense of place, a feeling for the old forms, and a loyalty to the past that no height of fame or degree of public adulation could ever compromise.

When she was a girl growing up in Fenwick, all athletics were in her province. She showed particular proficiency in golf. A fine golfer himself, my father recognized this talent in Kate. He used to play with her. She never forgot this. Late in her life, when she introduced me to someone, she would invariably say, "I used to play golf with his father." I assumed this was one reason she was so nice to me. She would remind me of it, too. She would remember him saying, "Come on, Kate, let's go play golf at Shenecossett" (forsaking Fenwick for a more seriously challenging course). She did not forget old friendships.

From her father, the doctor, she took her reddish complexion, her robust love of sport, and her fearlessness. He would quote to her from the prefaces of Shaw, the reigning playwright in the Hepburn household ("greater than Shakespeare").

In our talks, Kate revealed more about her home life. "When my mother and father were socially, slightly snubbed—just held a little at bay—for their political beliefs, I used to hang around Mr. Ingham. You remember Mr. Ingham and the fish house on the property I've bought?" She evoked the long-forgotten image of the incongruous little fishing shack in the sand dunes east of her house—on land adjoining her own which she had recently bought. "Yes, Mr. Ingham," she continued, "who later became the iceman when they pulled down his fishing shack as an eyesore. I used to run along the beach before all that part was filled in and out to the lighthouse to see Mr. Knowles, the lighthouse keeper, shouting to myself as I ran how I was going to save the world."

The image is compelling: the young Kate Hepburn, lithe and athletic, red-haired and freckled, running down the beach barefooted, away from home. Angry at the way she felt the conservative families of Hartford were thinking of her parents, she shouted her challenge, unheard, into the wind. She said, "I think powerful young girls have this sense that they're somehow going to save the world."

And at those teas on the Hepburn porch in my own boyhood, listening to Mrs. Hepburn and to whatever famous guest was present, I also felt the possibilities were all there and that somehow, in this world, I, too, would make my mark.

In the fall of 1940, as the presidential campaign heated up, the family naturally supported Franklin Roosevelt against the utilities lawyer Wendell Willkie. At one of the afternoon teas, I remember Kate telling the story of how she was invited to a rally of writers and artists for Roosevelt at Hyde Park. They would gather first at the house. Then the party would take place at Val-Kill, a favorite recreation place of the Roosevelts about two miles from the house, where a picnic would be laid out. Later, they would all participate in a radio program for Roosevelt. Prominent among the other expected guests was Edna Ferber, whose works were among the most popular of the time.

Ferber, as Kate recounted the story, got in touch with Kate in advance and offered to drive her up. They could go together, she said. Kate stalled, suspecting that Ferber didn't want Kate arriving alone and upstaging her. Instead of accepting the ride, Kate, by now thoroughly indoctrinated into airplane travel by her beau Howard Hughes, made plans to fly up to Hyde Park on her own. Her plane landed in the river. She clambered up the bank, getting muddied in the process, and made her way to the house. Entering by the front door, she met Roosevelt coming downstairs on the stairway elevator chair he used because of his crippling paralysis.

"Why, Kate!" he exclaimed on seeing her looking somewhat the worse for her unorthodox arrival. "Where have you been?"

Describing her plane ride and the landing in the river, she said she had wanted to beat Edna Ferber to the house. FDR laughed heartily. He obviously relished being the object of a competition between the two powerful women. The joke was a conspiratorial bond between him and Kate. When Edna Ferber arrived later, she was furious to see that Kate had preceded her and was now in cozy conversation with the president.

In that election, of course, Fenwick backed Willkie all the way—anyone but Roosevelt. They might well have also sided with Edna Ferber in her contest with the headstrong Hepburn.

Marion Hepburn Grant, in her book about Fenwick, tells two revealing stories of an encounter between her father and Morgan Gardner Bulkeley and one of her mother with Mrs. Bulkeley.

In the first, after "courteously greeting" the young doctor, Morgan Bulkeley, as treasurer of the borough, presented Dr. Hepburn with a bill for five hundred dollars for his part in the upkeep of the wooden bulkhead protecting all waterfront cottages. Dr. Hepburn was so taken aback that Bulkeley felt obliged to explain his philosophy of preserving Fenwick as a community. As Marion Grant described it, "As they talked, a mutual respect evolved between them. Each viewed the other and saw a real man. Dr. Hepburn cheerfully paid his share of the bill."

The second encounter between Mrs. Hepburn and Fannie Houghton Bulkeley, the widow of Morgan Bulkeley, took place over the women's vote. The two women, widely differing in their social and political views, especially women's suffrage, were distant cousins. Mrs. Bulkeley confessed that she had voted for the first time and was pleased to have done so. "I just wanted you to know that you were right and I was wrong," she said. After that, as Marion records the incident, the two women regarded each other with "a new affection."

My mother and Mrs. Hepburn had in common a sense of humor and a certain irreverence that cut across the prevailing New England sobriety. Yet my mother, unlike every other member of the family, seemed quite lost in Fenwick. As a blessing to me, the blazing sun on her light skin made beach life intolerable and she was apprehensive of the water as well. The summer storms that thundered down the river and out into the Sound to send occasional bolts of lightning sizzling on the bulkhead wall directly in front of our cottage terrified her and made her start and jump even before the bang. Tennis rather than swimming, sailing, or golf was more to her taste, but even here she was a reluctant participant.

In my mother's mind, there were other drawbacks to Fenwick. Twelve years younger than my father, socially, she was forced into a world more his than hers. At parties, this placed her continually in the company of older, dominant women, the wives of powerful Hartford business leaders who tended to treat her condescendingly as a younger sibling with a lot to learn. She found this unsettling and at times intimidating. Fenwick, she endured for the sake of her husband and children. I felt that while we were enraptured at being there, she got little pleasure out of the place herself.

One Fenwick activity that did give her pleasure was the ladies' bridge games, an established custom on midweek afternoons in those years in the 1930s. The game of two or three tables rotated among the cottages. Unconventional in so many other ways, Mrs. Hepburn was quite happy to adapt to the routines of this diversion. Her participation was not by any means to be taken as an attempt to ingratiate herself in an otherwise disapproving if not hostile community. It would have been completely foreign to her nature to make any concession of that sort. She simply enjoyed the game. Furthermore, she recognized that it served a useful social purpose in bringing together persons of differing temperaments and tastes who might otherwise have no common ground for communication. I felt that my mother and Mrs. Hepburn, although coming from different directions, were on the same side of the table—my mother with her feelings of inferiority among the wives of her husband's older friends, Mrs. Hepburn with her awareness of their distrust and disapproval of her ideas.

Always alert to what people thought and often defensive, my mother had a quick intelligence, although she had little book learning, and a wit that sometimes ran past her and verged on mockery. Towards her children, she had unlimited love and generosity. It was, I thought, an act of bravery and self-sacrifice that she endured Fenwick and all its trials for our sake.

In his mental makeup, my father was quite the opposite. Tenacious and thorough, appreciative of her humor but not himself witty and never caring what other people would think, he had a mastery of his complex business life. He was the chief officer of two vastly different companies at the same time, attending to one in the morning, the other in the afternoon.

While admiring this versatility in my father, I took it almost for granted. As children, this seemed a perfectly normal division of labor to us. In the morning, his office was on Park Street at the M.S. Little Manufacturing Company, makers of tubular brass plumbing goods, a company he had started himself. It was not a large company, but we were proud of it for having what in its day was the largest and best equipped foundry in Hartford. In the afternoon, he moved to his desk on Sigourney Street where he ran the Smyth Manufacturing Company, makers of world-famous book-binding machines, all of which, unlike the products of his own company, were priced in the many thousands of dollars. As children, we delighted in our visits to these companies. After attending to his correspondence, my father would give us a tour as a reward for waiting patiently. We would follow, for example, the manufacturing life of a shiny aluminum radiator valve ending with the stamping on the face of the valve of the diamond-shaped logo of the M.S. Little Manufacturing Company. Visits to the oily dark floors of the Smyth Company on Sigourney Street were a curiously different pleasure, viewing large, complex machines of intricate design whose end product was the binding of a book—a binding so skillful that it enabled a book when opened to lay flat.

In spite of his success and business acumen, what I grew to admire most in my father was his disciplined refusal to form quick personal judgments and his habit of always looking for the best qualities in other people.

His approach to his favorite game of golf was reflective of his character. He was not a natural player, as he would say. He was not born to the game but had taken it up in later life and was self-taught. Through patience and practice, he had mastered the game. It was said of him, "Mit Little may occasionally make a bad shot but he never in his life made a careless shot." I can see him under his visored cap address the ball, sight down the fairway, take a few practice golf stick waggles, and then execute the smooth, faultless, never-hurried swing. Ball after ball would go straight down the middle of the fairway. One never realized how remarkable this was—it seemed so effortless—until one tried to do it oneself. If he missed a shot, he hardly ever swore. He was apt to recall that Bobby Jones mastered the game only after conquering his temper. But occasionally, from under his breath, one could make out a faintly muttered, "Damn."

In all I did, I aspired to my father's command and self-control while admiring my mother's spontaneity and intuitiveness. Even this sort of objectivity required years to acquire, after many influences intervened, overriding those that came with growing up in Fenwick.

Chapter 8

After the War

The years immediately after the war brought in new people, and Fenwick began to change. One of those newcomers, in the summer of 1946, was my new wife, Anastazia, or "Stuzie" as her family called her. She first came to Fenwick five months after arriving in this country for the first time. She faced the usual curiosity, skepticism, and occasionally indifference of the Fenwick community. Marrying into Fenwick, however, was not the same as coming to Fenwick cold with no strings of attachment such as an in-law family already in place to pave the way. Stuzie, furthermore, had considerable plusses of her own. She was a blonde, lovely young Scandinavian of noble birth, born with the title of countess, and she had a new baby in her arms.

We had met under the chanciest circumstances in wartime London. In 1945, I was living in London in a flat at the end of Albemarle Street, off Piccadilly, with Jim Cross. We were both working for OSS (the Office of Strategic Services), predecessor to today's CIA. Nothing was ordinary about those times. Although I had the military rank of a sergeant, according to OSS custom I was in civilian clothes, the better to relate to British counterparts. My off-duty hours lacked any sort of military restriction or hindrance, except those that the bombardment of London by V-1's and V-2's imposed on the whole city.

At nine o'clock one evening in July 1945, I had my feet up in the living room of our flat when there was a knock on the door, and the slim figure of a young woman appeared. She was dressed in a black skirt and black fitted jacket over a white blouse. Her hair was blonde to the point of whiteness. The black suit, although looking somewhat war-worn, gave the appearance of smartness. The plain flat shoes she wore undercut the effect. This was Anastazia Lillie Marie Raben-Levetzau, who was just twenty-three.

She came asking for Jim. By military transport, she had recently arrived in London from her native country, Denmark, where she had been working for an American major in SHAEF (Supreme Headquarters Allied Expeditionary Force) in Copenhagen. In London, she was staying with an Englishwoman who had been a friend of the family in pre-war years. Before the war, Anastazia's family lived partly in England, partly in Denmark. A closed-up house in Wilton Street in Belgravia, untouched through successive bombardments of London, was waiting to be reopened when the war in Europe wound down and the family could come over. Because of her military connections, she was first in her family to get transport to London.

My roommate, who was assigned to the Danish section of the Special Operations Branch of OSS, had met the Raben family on a post-VE-Day trip to Denmark. He had left his London address with them. Stuzie, on reaching London, was searching for companions of her age. She had decided to look him up. As it turned out, it was simply my good fortune that Jim was out and I was in when she called.

I forget how I greeted her on that fateful evening. I think she, less surprised than I, carried the conversation. I know I tried to detain her, hoped to dispel her possible disappointment at not finding my roommate Jim. Something—not in myself or in the words we spoke—but something soon smoothed the edges of this unlikely encounter and made it seem inevitable. We moved into an easy intimacy. Five weeks after this meeting we were informally engaged to be married.

Soon I would face the arrival, one by one, from Denmark of members of her family: her father, her mother, and her sister, all eager to return to

London which they had left for Denmark as war was approaching. By this time, Jim Cross and I had moved into the large Upper Grosvenor Street flat maintained by a friend, Major Louis T. Stone, who was in military intelligence and needed replacements to share the high rent when his friend Walter Lord, later to become our friend as well, returned to Washington after OSS duty in London. The worldly Louis, seven years my senior, had told me, "Marry this girl and Hartford will never stop talking about it." He cautioned me to make sure I did nothing to alienate Stuzie's mother and sister when they arrived in London.

"If you lose the goodwill of either of those women," he said, "you will never marry Stuzie."

As it happened, her father was the first to secure travel papers and transport to London. Count Raben checked in at the Ritz Hotel in Piccadilly, and we met in his room before having dinner in the hotel dining room. My first view of my father-in-law-to-be was of a silhouetted figure seated at a desk in the frame of a window at the far end of the room. He gave us a glance over his glasses as we entered and then resumed writing a letter at the desk, explaining that he wouldn't be but a moment. In retrospect, I believe this was a premeditated kind gesture on his part, not to make the initial meeting too weighty an occasion and to allow the frightened suitor to look him over first and get used to his presence before we faced each other and shook hands. I was relieved and grateful. It was one of many gestures of kindness throughout the years.

Slight of build, Count Raben had an open, amusing face—a Danish face. He could never resist a joke, often one at his own expense, and that first dinner went easily. Mother and daughter, Pauline and Charlotte, reached London shortly afterward and removing the dust-cloth coverings from the furniture, went to work reopening the house in Wilton Street, which had been miraculously untouched by the war. My meeting with them was no more strained than it was with my father-in-law-to-be.

An only child, Pauline Raben was the product of one of those classic early twentieth century alliances between a moneyed upper-class American family and European nobility. Pauline looked to be a larger woman than she really was. Regarded by most people as quite formidable in her manner and physical presence, she was tall and big-boned but not large. She had a broad brow and a broad face with high, pronounced cheekbones and the widest, bluest eyes. My friend Lou Stone in London declared that she was "the most beautiful woman I ever saw."

Her mother was a Wheeler from Philadelphia, who was married very young to Count Maximillian Pappenheim from Bavaria. He was a member of a morganatic family distinguished also by having among its members a renowned general who fought in the Thirty Years War. Another time, this general had brutally suppressed a peasant revolt in upper Austria. He was cited by Heine in the often-quoted line, *"Ja, ich kenne meine Pappenheimer."* ("I know my Pappenheim.")

Leaving a very young bride and child, Max Pappenheim, noted for his good looks and irresponsible behavior, soon fled the marriage. Eventually, his gambling debts grew unmanageable, and he was banished even by his own family to take up an unknown exile in China where, it was supposed, he left a number of Asian Pappenheims.

The young, abandoned mother, hardly eager to return home to face Philadelphia society, took up residence in England, and Pauline was brought up in the indescribable peace of the English countryside with many of the privileges available to the child of a rich American mother bearing a notable European name.

For someone from Hartford, Connecticut, with inborn New England reserve, these new connections seemed strange and exotic. Yet living in wartime London was to be prepared for the unexpected: the morning and evening detonations of the V-2 rockets; the buzz bombs that chugged along their pilotless paths into the city. One mingled with Londoners seeking refuge in the Underground, encountered soldiers daily on the street in the uniforms of many different countries—all in a strange city that had come to seem home.

From the beginning and throughout our relationship, I never had a disturbing or awkward moment with my mother-in-law. Her total acceptance of me was an unaccountable gift. Unlike her daughter, she called me "Stu," not "Stuart," which seemed more intimate and made our relationship less formal. Stuzie suffered from what she felt was the unspoken disapproval of her mother most of her life and endured a wary, edgy mother-daughter relationship. I never felt any of that. As for Charlotte, five years younger than her sister, she became a conspiratorial friend.

Even now, however, I remember, with almost the same embarrassment and fascination I felt at the time, a premarital talk I had with my prospective father-in-law. In a kindly way, since I was young and away from home, he was acting in the place of my own father in inquiring about my experience with sex. Not appreciating the attitude of a worldly European, and not wishing to disclose the already begun sexual life I had with his daughter, I proclaimed total innocence, whereupon, quite easily, he lectured me gently on the need to be sure to satisfy the woman in a sexual relationship.

"One must not simply take one's own pleasure," he said.

His kindness did not prevent him from probing at the same meeting to discover the financial resources of my family since I, with an education still to complete, had none of my own. As if to test the waters, Count Raben reversed an old European marriage custom and suggested that I ask my father to settle a certain amount of money on the bride—a kind of reverse dowry. Chagrined, I explained this new and unique European custom to my New England father who, not without some skepticism, came up with a generous sum of money to satisfy the unapologetic count. The New World and the Old World had met.

Before the impending marriage, my father wrote me, "Stuzie certainly has a mixture of blood. Well, I guess our family needs it. As far as I know, at least on my side of the house and I think on your mother's, there is nothing but English blood. We are all probably too stolid and stodgy. Doubtless we need a little spice."

In September, the marriage took place in St. Margaret's Westminster, the very church where her parents were married twenty-seven years earlier, in 1918, at the end of the First World War. I was totally bound by English custom and Church of England marriage formalities, which included a sobering talk from Canon Don, the vicar of St. Margaret's and dean of Westminster Abby, and the posting of the banns on three successive Sundays at the church. The Rabens made much of the wedding of their elder daughter. They gave Stuzie three circular diamond pins. I received cuff links ringed with small diamonds and pearl shirt studs which I wore for the wedding.

The reception was at Claridge's Hotel, after which the married couple was driven forty-five minutes into the country to spend our one week of honeymoon as the guests of Margaretta Winchelsea, a family friend, beside the Sunningdale Golf Course. She had a supper already prepared for us. The kind hostess of our first married days, she left us largely alone to wander the golf course or read our books in the house. They were quiet days, in contrast to the rather accelerated pace of our short period of courtship.

That winter, Stuzie crossed to the United States aboard the Danish freighter *Falstria*. I was already home, having been discharged from military service. At the dock in Copenhagen, saying good-bye, her father had given her a delicate turquoise vase. Rolled up in the neck was a note in his hand, expressing a father's love, sending her on her way.

In that crossing, the ship's cargo had shifted in mid-voyage in the rough Atlantic. The listing of the ship in the angry winter seas made for an uncomfortable passage for my newly pregnant wife. Fortunately, she was crossing in the company of her Aunt Nina, a handsome, Boston-born American who had married a Count Moltke, a relative of my father-in-law. She was a splendid woman. She had a proud lift to her head that made her seem taller and more imposing than she was. Completely undaunted by the ship's difficulties, gallant Aunt Nina was a solicitous and calming companion on the trip, but her young niece ate little and arrived in her new country frail and ill, suffering from scurvy.

I had unaccountably misjudged the ship's arrival time in Hoboken and reached New York from Hartford to find her already located in Aunt Nina's Park Avenue hotel, where we met in confusion and embarrassment. Aunt Nina was kindly and welcoming despite my delinquency, but my parents, waiting in Hartford and monitoring the situation from there, were horrified at the unforgivable error of their son. Yet this miscue did not mar the ardor of our reunion.

We spent her first night in America at the midtown hotel residence of the parents of my friend Jim Cross and, after hiring a car, proceeded to

Hartford the following afternoon for the meeting with my parents. This meeting was doubly ceremonial. That evening, President Seymour of Yale, a college friend of my father's who was speaking at Hartford's Trinity College, was spending the night at our house. The long black limousine we had hired in New York rolled down our steep driveway and stopped under the porte-cochere at the front door. My father stepped out to welcome Stuzie with an embrace (and pay the driver from a sizeable wad of bills). I remember the scene, in our library that evening, of a somewhat dazed young Danish girl being the focus of attention. The president of Yale, more awesome to me than to her, engaged her in conversation about the war while my parents cast curious but, I thought, admiring eyes on the new family member.

It was in these moments, in the setting of my family home, that I began to realize the enormity of this event. A young woman had severed all connections with her past life, which in its way, but for the interruption of the war, had been as settled and conventional as mine. She had crossed the Atlantic to a new country where she knew only a handful of people to live with a foreign husband of very different background whom she had known for only six months.

As a new couple, we settled into the large east guest bedroom on Prospect Avenue to await the start of my accelerated senior year at Yale. Despite Stuzie's weakness from anemia and the morning sickness of her pregnancy, my mother was determined that we should have a party to celebrate the marriage and introduce my Danish bride to Hartford friends. My new bride did not relish the prospect of such an ordeal so soon after arriving in her new country. Her mother-in-law, on her side, hoped she would not show her pregnancy to Hartford society so few months after the marriage. Stuzie, doing her best to disguise her condition, rose to the occasion to greet the friends and endure a receiving line that lasted more than an hour.

Except for two of the guests, it all passed with relative smoothness. A Trinity College professor who spoke Danish tested her out in her native language and pronounced his disappointment with her accent. Apparently, he was disturbed by her overlay of British English, which she had spoken also from childhood.

Then, when Mrs. Hepburn came along, she appraised Stuzie closely and exclaimed, "I'm terribly disappointed. I expected Stuie to marry a fine, strapping Danish peasant girl."

When Mrs. Swain reached me in the receiving line, she spoke of her son Allen, my Fenwick friend, remembering the time we both had applied for the air force at the recruiting office in Hartford. I was disqualified because of astigmatism and allergies. Allen passed the tests. He did not return from the war.

A nice lot of silver and silver plate came our way as a result of this party, a perhaps not incidental part of my mother's overall design. Mrs. Hepburn's present to us was a toaster. "One can always use a toaster," she said sensibly. It served us daily for many years.

In those early days in Hartford, Dr. and Mrs. Hepburn befriended us, and we spent a number of pleasant evenings with them at their house on Bloomfield Avenue playing bridge. Coming from a gambling family, my wife was already proficient at the game; I was a novice.

"Now, Stuie," Mrs. Hepburn would say, laying down a scorecard at my place. "You've got to learn to score at the same time you learn to play." And we would play some hands, Mrs. Hepburn and me against the doctor and Stuzie. In this way, we all became friends until it was time to move to New Haven and resume classes at Yale.

The stay in New Haven was brief while I finished my foreshortened senior year. We found a room in an apartment above the Temple Street George and Harry's Restaurant that belonged to a Lithuanian woman named Mrs. Arbin. To reach our room, we had to walk through Mrs. Arbin's living room, but accommodations in this hectic post-war period, when everyone was intent on hurrying through and finishing up, were tight and there was little choice. It was not the sort of initial home to which I wanted to bring my pregnant young bride.

Entertaining there was cumbersome, but we tried it once or twice. One day, returning a courtesy in the Arbin living room, we invited to tea an English professor of mine, Benjamin Nangle, referred to behind his back as Ben, and his wife, who had been especially kind to us. Mrs. Arbin had a small terrier named Billy who was sometimes underfoot, especially when there was food on the table. The tea progressed somewhat stiffly. Stuzie, in her nervousness, drew the dog to her side, commanding, "Come here, Ben!" Professor Ben Nangle was momentarily startled. As Stuzie later described the unfortunate moment, "His walleye jumped." The story went around the English Department.

Graduation came in June, as did Caroline Little, and mother and baby took up residence in Fenwick. In later years, Fenwick, for Stuzie as always for me, the house and the place, became a real home—far more so than the small cooperative apartment house we landed in in New York, which in spite of our living there for thirty-two years always seemed somehow transitory and temporary. Fenwick was the fixed point.

At about the same time my Danish-born wife arrived in Fenwick, a Hartford entrepreneur came to town. His appearance strangely echoed that of Edward Stokes seventy-five years earlier. Stokes, in his yacht, came to buy Fenwick Hall and turn the hotel into a smart seaside resort. E. Clayton Gengras came to buy the Riversea Inn. This columned mansion was the modern-day equivalent of Fenwick Hall and was located not a hundred yards south on Fenwick Avenue from the site of Fenwick Hall. Gengras was later to introduce to an awed Fenwick the only yacht in local ownership large enough to rival that of Stokes' *Fra Diablo*. But his plans for Fenwick were later to cause not only controversy but also acrimonious divisions within the community.

Clayton Gengras was a handsome, charming, hugely energetic businessman of mercurial temperament who was to beat the Hartford insurance executives at their own game and become one of Hartford's richest citizens—and, later on, one of its most generous benefactors as well. He got his start as a Ford dealer and rode the postwar prosperity. He turned his dealership into one of the most successful in New England. In 1948, for his family of ten children, he bought and remodeled a Fenwick cottage on a high bluff overlooking the South Cove. In the late 1950s, he moved into insurance and prospered. In 1966, he was to run for governor on the

Republican ticket—shades of Morgan G. Bulkeley—but in this endeavor, unlike all his other pursuits including golf on the Fenwick course, he was to encounter a rare defeat.

Shortly after acquiring the inn and some adjacent properties in 1943, Gengras applied for a liquor license for the inn. Up to this point, the Riversea had been run in what senior Fenwick citizens might have considered quiet good taste. The inn's proprietors respectfully embraced local New England customs, attracting certifiably New England customers, and ingratiating themselves with the community by conducting open weekly dances to which all ages were welcome. Calling for a liquor license was as shocking to Fenwick as importing topless dancers to entertain at Saturday night dances.

Gengras's application split the community. Marion Hepburn Grant, younger sister of Katharine, was among those opposed, and there was no reticence in Marion when her sense of justice was offended. I loved this in Marion. At times, she could be exasperating in her certainties and in her persistence. She was always pursuing some civic-minded plan, and she was tireless in attempting to draw one into the orbit of her enthusiasms. In the liquor license controversy, my father, in quieter fashion but just as tenaciously, was at her side and appeared with her before the State Liquor Commission in Hartford. By the time they reached the hearing, they suspected that the case was already lost and that Gengras had the votes in his pocket. They were right.

At the height of the liquor controversy, my father, Marion, and their allies risked some long-standing friendships. Even within the same family, there were divisions—pro-Gengras and anti-Gengras sentiment. Bystanders such as myself were caught up in the we/they emotion of the crisis descending on our little community like a sudden summer thunderstorm.

Some of the fireworks went off a block away from us when Uncle Hought, as warden, held a community meeting in his front yard to air the dispute. An obviously aggrieved and defensive Gengras at one point erupted in anger. He was chastised by a stern, scowling Warden. But in his quest for Fenwick property was Clayton doing anything more than others had done before him—carving out his piece of the world? Were his tactics any different than those used by everyone else, my father not excepted, when there was advantage to be gained? For my father and his friends, the pushy period was over. Their gains were settled and accepted. Time had cloaked them in respectability. They had joined with history. Clayton, the newcomer, was still to prove himself. Meanwhile, his every motive was suspect. One was tempted to assign a label to this disruptive force in our midst. He was the outsider and, furthermore, he was an interloping Catholic among Protestants.

Part of the suspicion of Gengras was indeed this New England suspicion of the Catholic. Fenwick had a strong tradition of Anglican Protestantism. The Fenwick chapel and the ritual of eleven o'clock Sunday services had their origins in the living room of Francis Goodwin's cottage in the 1880s. When these services became too crowded, in 1885, Goodwin, an amateur architect (and, incidentally, a friend of the great Hartford-born planner Frederick Law Olmsted), designed and built his own small chapel on a neighboring lot. The following year, enlarged and with a bell tower, it was moved to its present location on what is now the first fairway of the Fenwick golf course.

In tiny Fenwick, no fewer than four Episcopal bishops have owned or lived in cottages, and the place has been home to four Episcopal priests, five if you count Katharine Hepburn's paternal grandfather, an occasional visiting preacher. This strong Episcopal presence is mitigated somewhat by a surviving strain of Congregationalism, the early dominant religious denomination of New England and a church harboring even greater suspicions of Catholicism than the Episcopalians. From the start, however, Francis Goodwin intended that the chapel services should be non-denominational (although not so non-denominational as to encourage Catholicism). His injunction to keep matters ecumenical was designed to prevent rivalries between Fenwick families that perhaps already existed on other grounds—social, political, or economic—from entering the religious realm. Over the course of the summer, the choice of visiting ministers to conduct the Sunday services reflected the loyalties of each constituency. The Episcopalians, who had charged themselves with the management of affairs at St. Mary's by the Sea, were always tactful about keeping an equitable balance between Congregational and Episcopalian.

My family lined up on the Congregational side. Mother and Father bowed their heads in prayer from a seated position, not descending to the kneeling cushions provided. But in myself, I felt the division keenly. I was brought up in the severe, starkly plain Old South Church in Hartford and was sent away to the Reverend Endicott Peabody's Episcopal Church school, Groton School in Groton, Massachusetts. There I attended morning prayer every school day for five years in a Gothic chapel whose size bore about the same relationship to the community it served as Salisbury Cathedral does to its town in Wiltshire.

Groton was then thought to be a snobbish school. Among all those form-mates from New York or Boston, I worried about my status coming from Hartford. But the snobbishness I developed was mainly religious. I was being shaped into an Episcopalian by the regular chapel-going and frequent prayer periods. And in time, the Episcopal liturgy seemed superior to the plainspoken Congregationalism of my parents. Yet the Puritanism of my background still clung to me, even when I, too, became a New Yorker and my focus as a journalist became the presumably wicked Broadway theater.

The contentious issue of the inn was finally resolved when a group of borough residents put up the money in 1949 to buy the property from Gengras and rezone it as residential. It became a family residence in 1959 and has remained in private hands ever since. With his acquisition of a Fenwick cottage in 1948, Gengras and his family became more and more a part of the community. Two of his children in time intermarried with one of Fenwick's oldest families and, in fact, into the very Episcopal family that had assumed the management of chapel affairs since the days of the Reverend Francis Goodwin.

In the summer of 1946, our life in Fenwick was formal and ceremonial. We were not on our own. My father and mother presided over the cottage, and Pauline, my mother-in-law, had come over for the birth and was staying with us. There was also in residence a temporary nurse for the new baby to shepherd us through the early days. Fenwick provided breathing room, but we also had restrictions and of an altogether different kind. The house was full and was run on an exact schedule. For the young married couple with a new baby, there were a lot of grown-ups to answer to. Having Pauline there too was worrying to us both. How would she get on with my parents? Sometimes formidable, Pauline was not intimidating to my father, but I wondered how my mother felt in her presence.

Stuzie was eager for her mother to meet the only friends she could then count on in Fenwick, the senior Hepburns we had seen in Hartford. This was easily accomplished. All one had to do was show up for one of the regular daily afternoon teas on the Hepburn porch.

From her post behind the tea table, with family and friends gathered around, she encouraged self-expression and applauded any declaration of opinion. It was as if she cast a spotlight on the inspired speaker, even when the expression of opinion was outrageous and calculated to annoy. When my austere-looking mother-in-law was introduced by her name, Countess Raben, Dick, the oldest son, set up a mocking chant, "Oh, is it cock robin, cock robin?" Mrs. Hepburn, making no move to rescue the moment, sat there with a fixed smile and waited him out. My mother-in-law seethed.

Nevertheless, Dick became a true friend to Stuzie and me, a part of our summers. He would come by on his bicycle or in his red truck and sit himself down in our kitchen usually accepting a cup of tea. It took very little to get him started. Visits from Dick were occasions of high hilarity. He always had tales to tell—about his latest maneuvers to get a play of his read by, or into the hands of, an actress of note, a director, or a producer; about someone who had come to stay overnight and had remained for a week (the Hepburns were famously generous hosts to casual visitors); about a character in town who had supplied Dick with a character in his latest play script; and, best of all, about his sister Kate.

He talked about his sister—"the living legend"—with a mixture of pride and deprecation that suggested an old sibling rivalry was still alive. But in Dick's presence, it was wise not oneself to be too anxious to agree. Observing Kate's behavior when she came to Fenwick after having finished a run in a play, Dick developed a theory about actors just off a run: public adulation and nightly applause are like a drug to which one becomes addicted. Withdrawal symptoms inevitably accompany the sudden ending of the stimulus—the closing of the play—bringing episodes of irritability, rudeness, discontent, and even cruelty. About the time the curtain is due to come down and the applause could be expected to begin, the actress, now idle, exhibits such signs. Dick would act out Kate in these circumstances, with self-pitying sighs and gestures. The effect would be exaggerated on a matinee day when the out-of-work actress would be deprived of the love, adulation, and applause of not one audience but two.

Dick noted also that the actress continued to play scenes even after the play had ended. A favorite scene would be a confrontation scene, played with anyone near at hand, usually, Dick felt, himself.

Dick took dead aim at the weaknesses and vulnerabilities of the characters in all his tales. And one didn't get off scot-free oneself. He would mimic Stuzie speaking inaudibly through nearly closed lips. He would mock my own stuffiness and reserve. All his teasing and stories and mimicry were accompanied by wild, derisive laughter. The experience of his visits set up vibrations that lasted for days.

In later years, Dick lived on in that big house courtesy of Kate and wrote his plays and kept his journals, jotting notes of everything that transpired around him. He roamed far afield from Fenwick, knew the river valley, and discovered walks in the woods of Old Lyme. He made friends with local Saybrook characters, the more eccentric, the more to his liking. One envied him his enjoyment of accidental happenings, the value he put on nature, his free spirit. One examined one's own restricted life with its small, worldly concerns and then Dick's embrace of freedom and wondered why.

To return to our early years together in Fenwick, for Stuzie, the reception had been smooth. The Hepburns were quick to adopt a newcomer to Fenwick. The less newcomers had in common with the run of Fenwickians, the better. To just the degree they were shunned by the community at large, so were they embraced by the Hepburns. If the Hepburns had been around when Edward Stokes and his notorious New York friends had made their forays into Fenwick, they would have found at least one ally in the borough.

In no Hepburn was this contrary streak better illustrated than in Kate. When Katharine Hepburn in 1983 was about to make her forty-fifth, and last, feature-length film in and around New York, I followed its progress. (My proposed book never jelled.) The financial underpinning of the project, which was in the hands of Cannon Films, a company then better known for exploitation films than for high cinema art, was dubious. "The situation could be chaotic," she said. "The project is so uncertain. It's been on-again, off-again so many times. Cannon Films apparently owes money all over town." Yet, she was attracted to the Cannon producers, Menahem Golum and Yorum Globus.

Kate and her director, Tony Harvey, had ongoing arguments with them. In fact, Kate had to put up some of her own money to get the project going and then had to fight her producers to be rewarded with points in the production commensurate with her investment. Still, despite their reputations and the pre-production acrimony, Kate was fascinated with Golem and Globus. "They have the kind of energy I admire," she said.

In much the same way, Kate felt at home with a film crew—the gaffers, the electrics, the soundmen, and the grips with ponytail hairdos and wide leather wrist bracelets. "It's funny," she said to me, "how certain professions attract certain types of people. Everyone in this business is a little crazy … gypsies … not quite respectable. Have you noticed? They're all just a little bit 'off.'"

The Hepburns, I thought, accepted Stuzie so readily because she, too, was thought to be a little bit "off." Dr. Hepburn called her "fey." A man of gruff exterior, he was kind to her. One day, he took her aside. "You're not well, are you?" he said. Some months later, in New York, she had an emergency gall bladder operation that revealed a condition that had existed unknown to her since childhood.

Stuzie was "off," maybe, out of the ordinary to be sure, possibly eccentric in the manner the Hepburns themselves were thought to be. In spite of that, she took easily to Fenwick people and they quickly to her.

Chapter 9

Apart from Fenwick

When I was about to take on my main newspaper job—writing a daily column on theater—three Fenwick friends, each one an actress—came to mind. They were the only theater persons I knew. Foremost, of course, was Katharine Hepburn, but I couldn't bother her with questions. She existed as pure inspiration—and an encouraging example of rebelling against the prevailing Fenwick business orientation. I could talk to Hopie Bulkeley, one of my sister's earliest childhood friends and my playmate as well, who lived a Fenwick block away. Hope Cameron, as she came to be known professionally, was a member of Actors' Studio and had been a member of the original cast of *Death of a Salesman*. She gave me a list of books to study (I was a delinquent student) and a good piece of advice: Never attack the person of the actor because then you compromise an actor's entire livelihood; only criticize the actor in the role. As I read drama critics later, those words rang in my ear.

The third Fenwick actress, Rosemary, came to Fenwick and bought a cottage largely because one summer she stayed with us while playing Lady Macbeth at the American Shakespeare Festival in Stratford, Connecticut, and came to love the place. Having had a rich theater career, she was a valuable source of information to a neophyte theater journalist.

I was trained on the old *New York Herald Tribune.* Upon arriving in New York in the fall of 1946 with a wife and small baby, Caroline, I bought a two-bedroom cooperative apartment for $6,000 which was located in a small building on busy East Sixtieth Street opposite the loading platforms of Bloomingdale's. The building was slightly finer than its backdoor business surroundings. A Mediterranean-style stucco façade with balconies covered what originally were two brownstones joined together, making for a distinct stylistic separation, for instance, from the Subway Bar at the Lexington Avenue corner. For a neighbor, we boasted Eugene Speicher, the preeminent New York portrait painter of the day. He and his attractive wife, Elsie, befriended us and shared stories of their high life. In one such story, Speicher told how he once painted a crusty Texas mogul and traveled to Dallas for the unveiling. His Texas subject warned him that he'd accept the painting only if his little dog on seeing the portrait gave a bark of recognition. At the appropriate moment, Elsie Speicher gave the dog a judicious kick. It barked in reply, and the sale was assured.

Taking tentative steps in New York, we looked to Fenwick as our true home. Determined to make a place for myself in the newspaper business, I found a job as copy boy making thirty-five dollars a week on the old *New York Herald Tribune.* In the career climb upwards, my first mentionable job was as assistant New York correspondent for the European Edition of the *Herald Tribune.* Later I would become editor, with the task of preparing a daily budget of news to send overseas by teletype. Periodically, the Paris-based boss of the *Tribune*-owned paper, Geoffrey Parsons Jr., would make a New York visit. During our informal business chats in Bleeck's, the bar downstairs and out the back door of the building, I was ever hopeful of getting the nod and being summoned to Paris to live the expatriate's life. It never happened.

Despite my lowly starting job as a copy boy, I had a moment of distinction. I hoped it did not escape the notice of higher authorities on the paper when I was called upon to describe my work as a copy boy on a Voice of America broadcast beamed to the Soviet Union. That came about because an American cousin of my wife, Charles W. Thayer, was the head of the Russian unit of the Voice in New York.

Trying to think of a possible new skill to lift myself above copy boy in the journalistic world, we had called upon Thayer to see if he could arrange Russian lessons. He put us together with a charming Russian lady new to New York and new to the English language. Nina Alexeva and her husband Kyril, with two small children, had fled his economic attaché post in Mexico to seek asylum in the United States. This early defection made the front page of *The New York Times*. In a home-and-home language arrangement, we were to teach Nina English and she would teach us Russian. Under the mistaken impression that after a few lessons, I had a certain familiarity with the language, Thayer summoned me to the studio to record my democratic message to the Russian people.

Without mastering Russian, I made my way up through the ranks of rewriteman, reporter, and assistant city editor. In that latter capacity, I was virtually in charge of the paper on weekends, and if a big newsbreak came, I was subject as well to inquiry calls from the severe Mrs. Whitelaw Reid, the owner of the paper, the ever-present possibility of which had me quaking in anticipation.

Sensing that in television there was something even more wonderful than newspaper life, after five years, I left the paper for NBC. After journeyman work on a local news program, I got a job as an assistant writer in the documentary unit headed by Henry Solomon. He was in high favor at NBC, his unit commanding considerable prestige because of the success of his *Victory at Sea*. This skillfully produced record of the war in the Pacific had a distinguished musical score by Richard Rodgers.

In the unit, I shared an office with the famous Broadway musical arranger Robert Russell Bennett who was responsible for the scores of countless shows by Rodgers and Hammerstein, Cole Porter, George Gershwin, Irving Berlin, and others. Rodgers had supplied the grand sweeping themes of *Victory at Sea*, but it was Bennett, I learned, who put it all together behind film and conducted the NBC Symphony Orchestra at the recording sessions.

I was fascinated by his method. With a film shot list to follow, Russell worked simultaneously down and across the notation page, arranging each instrument's music vertically and running the theme horizontally across the page, all to the shot list.

Russell had a small upright piano in the office that he used primarily to summon pretty secretaries down the hall, playing a different tune for each one. He confided in me, his admiring but curious office mate, that his musical flirtations did not signify any serious involvements. "Oh," he said dismissively, "I might pat a luscious breast or two, but that's all."

Bennett was more serious about visiting the racetrack. In the afternoons, he would disappear from the office, racing form in hand, to place his bets at Aqueduct. He overcame an awkward swaying limp in his walk, traceable to early polio, to play hard games of tennis at Forest Hills. He was a tall, elegant man, unfailingly kind and considerate, and a wonderful companion for all-too-limited a time.

In the office, my first job was to work on a documentary on the atomic bomb entitled *Three, Two, One, Zero*. I was proud of my one significant contribution to the script of that show. Against the figures of badly burned victims of Hiroshima, I found the words in *King Lear* to accompany the images of the deeply scarred people:

> Poor naked wretches, wheresoe'er you are,
> That bide the pelting of this pitiless storm,
> How shall your houseless heads and unfed sides,
> Your loop'd and window'd raggedness, defend you
> From seasons such as these?

Working for Henry Solomon had pleasurable detours. Four of us in the unit sailed first-class aboard that elegant liner the *United States* on a European trip to select film from archives in London and Paris for the next project, a documentary on the Soviet Union. With the confidence and full backing of the highest executive level of NBC, our unit lived well on its generous expense account, sampling the menus of the best Parisian restaurants, beginning with the pressed duck at Tour d'Argent.

In Paris, however, I grew sicker and sicker on rich restaurant food until I was finally reduced to my hotel bed. I could hardly face a room service dinner of poached sole and a pear without feelings of nausea. I was diagnosed with hepatitis and shipped off to the American Hospital in Neuilly. The recovery period there extended to three weeks including Thanksgiving before I was discharged to fly home for further recovery in my own bed on Sixtieth Street.

The drawn-out illness caused the complete disruption of my career in television. My NBC superiors were understanding and helpful, and when I recovered sufficiently, I returned to the news division to write the eleven o'clock local news with John K.M. McCaffery. The effects of the depressing and debilitating disease lingered for a year, and I lost momentum in the drive to find success in what was then the promising and chic advance post of journalism.

At the end of the 1950s, an unexpected call came from my old employer, the *New York Herald Tribune*. They asked if I would be interested in writing the daily theater news column. I found this a surprisingly hopeful prospect: my own column in the paper five days a week. I had seen enough of television. Like motion pictures as opposed to live theater, television was a derivative news purveyor; newspapers for all their antiquity were primary.

My start on my new job was not auspicious. I thought to call on a theater producer or two, to put a toe in the water, as it were. In the confusion of those days, I was abashed to find myself almost an hour late for my first appointment with Kermit Bloomgarden.

In the list of producers I had some familiarity with Bloomgarden occupied a reverential place. Understandingly nervous making my late entrance to his office, I found it in a low, typically shabby-looking Times Square building whose entire street façade was covered by a vast advertising sign. Within the sign itself, incongruously, one window was cut. That window provided the only daylight in Bloomgarden's office.

Sitting in artificial light, the producer of Arthur Miller's *Death of a Salesman* and *The Crucible*, Lillian Hellman's *The Autumn Garden* and *Toys in the Attic*, Meredith Willson's *The Music Man*, and of *The Diary of Anne Frank* and *Equus*, greeted me kindly. At first, his rather severe look of appraisal was disturbing, but he made little of my lateness, and we had our talk.

He described the function of a producer in matter-of-fact terms. Bloomgarden's preparation for theater was as an accountant. At a union contract negotiation he once attended, a prominent labor lawyer volunteered his definition of a producer: "A producer is a businessman with artistic pretensions."

An angry Bloomgarden rose to his feet. "No, a producer is an artist with business pretensions."

Impossible as it may seem now, the *Trib* in those days was fully competitive with *The New York Times*, and, indeed, a feared rival. Writing the theater news column, however, made me conscious of how outnumbered by the *Times* we on the *Tribune* were. I was competing against three daily theater news reporters on the *Times*—the feared Sam Zolotow, who made theater people quake when his rasping, demanding voice came over the telephone; Arthur Gelb, biographer, along with his wife Barbara, of Eugene O'Neill, later to become managing editor of the *Times*; and Louis Calta. Each took turns writing the daily column. And in the Sunday theater section, Lewis Funke was competing against all of us for news. Because producers preferred to appear in the *Times*, the hard news would flow to the competition. I realized I had to do something different. They worked the phone. I had to get out, walk the streets, and knock on doors.

Early in my days on the job, I encountered Elia Kazan for the first time. In the 1960s, no names in the theater were more honored than those of Elia Kazan and Tennessee Williams, and both came together in an early column I wrote about Williams' *Sweet Bird of Youth*. In the second week of rehearsal, I caught up with Kazan, who was directing the play, at the Rooftop Theater above the New Amsterdam on West Forty-Second Street, a space briefly famous in the 1920s when Eddie Cantor, Maurice Chevalier, and Ruth Etting performed there in the Midnight Frolics. Later, the theater fell into disuse until the early days of television. The camera ramp still jutted out into the audience. In this dark, dusty, and neglected space, now only utilized for occasional play rehearsals, I introduced myself to Kazan, using the name of a friend we had in common.

Still green in my job, I asked him how he thought theater should be covered.

He answered me unhesitatingly. "Just write what you see," he said.

This was the confirmation I was looking for. Go backstage and see what lies behind. In my column the next day, after setting the stage of the incongruent location, I wrote:

> Just before the midday break, Geraldine Page and Paul Newman played the first scene of the first act of *Sweet Bird of Youth* for Elia Kazan. Miss Page spoke a monologue lasting nearly five minutes, a list of instructions for her new young stage companion, Paul Newman. As he must, he sat silently with hands folded through the scene, rising only at the end.
>
> In his director's chair, Mr. Kazan sat no less silently, not once breaking the mood of the scene with instructions. Once, he turned to a pad on a table and made a note. All the instructions for the actors he saved for the end.

Writing what you saw required the recognition of promising occasions such as the first rehearsal of a new production coming in. First rehearsals generally took place in a theater (often the theater booked for the play) or a rehearsal hall. Usually, the producer had a few words of welcome expressing high expectations for everyone's success. The director might well give his thoughts about the theme and style of the play. I would have some quotes to enliven the column from this opening. The lead didn't always have to be: "The first reading of such-and-such a play took place today in such-and-such a theater (rehearsal hall)." Something would happen or something would come out of talking to the producer or an actor or the director to give the story some life. I remember encountering Richard Rodgers in a Times Square rehearsal hall at the opening rehearsal day of a revival of his *Babes in Arms*. I mentioned knowing his daughter Mary, who had an early success in theater with her musical *Once Upon a Mattress*. His response was, "Yes, I think she has the necessary talent, drive, and ability to get along with people to have a career." In his ascending scale of priorities was an important recognition of the collaborative nature of theater.

I had to keep looking for backstage opportunities that would throw a spotlight on the working life of the theater. It was my curiosity concerning a world I knew nothing about that prompted me, I suppose, to examine more closely the process of making theater. The creative aspects of theater became more interesting to me than the end result. The fully staged final version of the play I had seen evolving in these backstage visits often came as a disappointment. It was not an uncommon experience in theater. Ironically, a play in its rough state, before costumes and scenery have been added, enacted against a bare stage, often looked better to theater people than it did at its fully dressed opening.

I was right to follow Kazan's suggestion and my own instincts and try to see as much of the theater as I could. The strategy also entailed showing up at the offices of producers to see what news could be squirreled out of them before the *Times* got it. In that way, I came to know a remarkable group of men—besides Kermit Bloomgarden, David Merrick, the most prolific producer of his day; Alexander H. Cohen, the canniest of show promoters; Harold Prince, whose youthful zest for the business was irresistible; Robert Whitehead, a thoughtful but daring champion of serious work; Roger L. Stevens, a real estate magnate turned dogged producer, often Whitehead's partner; Cheryl Crawford, a quiet fighter for the dramatic arts; Leland Hayward, the self-assured begetter of big ideas, one of which became *South Pacific*; Alfred de Liagre, the aristocratic model of a Broadway producer—a varied but fascinating lot.

One of the unexpected pleasures of the job was bringing this world into Fenwick. I had a reader in Fenwick. He was Uncle Hought—Houghton Bulkeley. Uncle Hought was a reader and a loyal friend.

I had no way of realizing it at the time, but I had come into the business at a peak period in the life of the independent producer on Broadway. The 1960s might well have marked the high point. After the sixties, the continually escalating production costs resulted in a muddling of the producer's function. It took a consortium to put on a show. When the musical *42nd Street* opened on Broadway in 1980, only one producer was listed in the program: David Merrick. In the 2001 revival, eleven names were in his place above the title. Producing had come to resemble a multi-corporate partnership, and something has been lost. There was a distinctive, identifiable look to the productions of any of the gentlemen named. This was a Merrick show; that was a Prince, or that was a de Liagre. Today, such distinctions are blurred in the dispersion of responsibility.

Arthur Cantor was one of those independent producers, fearless and combative, and he continued doggedly so until almost the end of his life, complaining about and cursing the business he loved, to become one of the last of this frequently cantankerous breed. On visits to Fenwick, Arthur liked to relax on our west porch, which he named "the Dreyfus porch," because its modern renovation had been paid for largely out of the generous earnings I had made helping Jack Dreyfus write his book about the way his life had been changed by the miracle drug Dilantin. Arthur, always ready with a pun, called it, "Da magic Dilantin."

A Harvard-educated, literate man and a student of the Bloomsbury Set, he was enormously curious and gregarious, and yet a man known in the business as a hard, close-fisted bargainer. He was also to become one of my closest friends. It was an unlikely friendship to be sure, but a close one nevertheless. Shortly after I started on my new job as theater news reporter for the *Tribune*, when I was especially aware of my own limitations for the job, Arthur took me to lunch at the Harvard Club. In the ensuing hour or so, as he talked about the theater and its personalities, I had a course in Broadway more comprehensive than anything I learned in my next several eye-opening months on the job. Arthur was to have a greater influence on the future course of my life than I could have anticipated at the time.

I quickly succumbed to the charms of a daily byline. I could count on my parents as devoted readers. My presence in the paper signaled to them that I had survived the dangers of another day in New York City. My father, taking the long view, had looked on my newspaper career in larger terms.

My greatest success in school and college had been my election as chairman of the *Yale Daily News*, a position my father had also held in his day at Yale. This lifted me above the daily newspaper grind into a lofty editorial chair. It was a position of some power on campus, and I suppose I became enamored of my privileged place. This of course would never be duplicated in later life, but I suppose in my deeper unconscious, I was always reaching for it. Perhaps I was also troubled by an ambivalence in my thinking traceable to the influence of my father in opposition to my own inclinations—whether, like him, I wanted to be the acting executive and manage important affairs or stay on the outside as the observer, the reporter and writer. Or could I somehow combine the two? On the one hand, there was the steadfast certainty of my father's life work, which I by turns admired and discounted, and on the other, the uncertain line of my own, with which I was untrusting and impatient.

He thought the best opportunities for a newspaperman lay in writing a syndicated national column such as the one Joseph and Stewart Alsop wrote. Mine wasn't that, but it was a column, and it was my own.

It all ended when the *Tribune* went out of business one day in 1966. On that dire day, Blaine Littell, a friend on the paper, and I retreated to the Century Association on West Forty-Third Street, where we were members, to drown our sorrow. Skipping lunch entirely, we proceed straight to the bar. We took our glasses to the billiard room downstairs, refueling from time to time, to play some blurry pool throughout the long afternoon.

Now the question was what to do next. The seven years I wrote the column seemed like a long span of time. The work was unrelenting and intensive. I loved it, even if it meant always worrying about coming up each day with a respectable column by the 6:00 PM deadline. I had intended to continue as a newspaperman with the *Tribune* indefinitely. Now I had an idea for a news magazine of the theater. A new idea always seems promising until the first contradictory opinion comes along. When Clay Felker, the talented creator of *New York* magazine, heard of my plans, he said he hoped it wouldn't be a theater magazine. His point was that theater, intrinsically, could not generate enough advertising to support a magazine. I thought I could overcome this drawback by structuring the magazine as a subscriber inducement for the growing cluster of regional theaters that was then emerging.

To work out my idea, I had the help of several friends. My theater friend Arthur Cantor provided me with a rent-free room in his producing office in the Sardi Building. On the business side, I had the counsel of my college friend Walter Curley, a partner in J.H. Whitney & Company, later to become ambassador to Ireland and then France. He guided me in putting together a financial proposal to accompany a produced dummy of the magazine to take to money sources.

Arthur's Sardi Building office consisted of a number of rooms along a corridor, one of which contained an early model keyboard-driven machine called a computer. I had never heard of such a thing, had no idea what it did, and stayed well away. Arthur was enthralled with all forms of gadgetry, although he often had some difficulty manipulating them.

Arthur occupied the front room just inside the entrance. At the far end of the corridor as a subtenant was his good friend, the agent Bobby Sanford, who represented, among others, the playwright Paddy Chayefsky. Arthur produced some of Chayefsky's best plays: *The Tenth Man*, *Gideon*, and *The Passion of Josef D.* Sanford endowed me with a name, "Stewy-boy," that carried some Yiddish connotation out of the Bronx, and Arthur thereupon took to calling me Stewy-boy, not without affection, but in some amusement at its application to a New England-born WASP.

Right after the *Tribune* closed its doors, I got a call from John F. Wharton, a founding partner of the law firm of Paul, Weiss, Rifkind, Wharton, and Garrison. I knew him from my theater reporting days. He was a statesmanlike figure in the theater, and he was thoroughly immersed in it, handling theater business for the firm, counseling the Playwrights' Company, acting as a trustee of the Cole Porter estate. He represented such heavyweight clients as Marshall Field, the *Chicago Sun Times*, and Norman Cousins of *Saturday Review*. A new theater organization, the Theatre Development Fund, was in formation, and he invited me to join the founding board. TDF, thanks in part to the sponsorship and management of TKTS, the half-price ticket booth in Times Square, was in time to become the largest nonprofit organization in the performing arts. I remained connected with it throughout.

Wharton also took a lively interest in the magazine. He sent me to a couple of contacts of his. One introduction led to Norman Cousins, who said he thought my proposal in words and figures was one of the best magazine proposals he had seen. That was nice, but that was all. (Subsequently, I was to strike out a second time with Norman Cousins. His managing editor, Richard Lardner Tobin, whom I knew from *Tribune* days, got me to write a column on books in publishing for a monthly section of the magazine. I wrote this column for a couple of years in my post-*Tribune* freelance years. Then the job of assistant managing editor, with the eventual prospect of succeeding Tobin, became vacant. Dick proposed me for the job, believing the selection was his to make. Not so. Cousins, with a candidate of his own, moved in, and I lucked out again.)

Another referral provided by Wharton led straight to Gustave L. Levy, then managing partner of Goldman Sachs. His office was at the end of a large open room from which he looked out on rows of desks belonging, I assumed, to the trading partners of the firm. Gustave Levy was a short, high-spirited, impatient man full of motion. He did not devote any extra time to my presentation. Behind his desk lay an open briefcase. With a sweep of his arm, he pitched my proposal into his bag, a clean hoop shot. "I'm going to California this evening to see Norton Simon," he said. "Perhaps he'll be interested." I recognized Simon's name as being as golden in financial circles as Levy's own. I had hit the big time … or else I was in way over my head. I heard nothing further either from Mr. Levy or Mr. Simon.

I next called on Richard Rodgers with whom I had a newspaper friendship. He reacted favorably and sent me to his financial man to work out the details. One necessity was made clear from the outset—Rodgers was willing to put up the entire sum estimated for the project (in the neighborhood of a quarter of a million dollars) but, I assumed for tax reasons, he required that he be an eighty percent partner. By this time, I was in discussions with a business partner who operated a successful gardening magazine and wanted to expand his holdings. He balked at Rodgers' terms. At that, the project, to which I had devoted nearly a year, collapsed.

I was to remain in the limbo world of freelance work until 1986, when I resigned as a board member and joined the staff of the Theatre Development Fund. I thought it should be represented by a regularly appearing newsletter. I joined the staff to create one and was on a payroll again.

Along the way, I had become editor of the *Authors Guild Bulletin*—a job that called for four or five days of work quarterly and led, indirectly, to another project involving an association with William F. Buckley Jr., one of several major personalities I encountered on my uncertain journey.

The first was Senator Mark O. Hatfield of Oregon. Arthur Cantor again came to my assistance. Arthur picked up friends on his travels. In that way, he met Gerald W. Frank, a scion of the Meyer & Frank department store family in Portland and now Senator Hatfield's chief of staff. Jerry Frank felt Hatfield should have a book to burnish an already shining political career. He was in a position to finance it out of his own pocket. Arthur suggested me as the writer. We interested Evan Thomas of Harper & Row in the project, and he suggested a title, *Not Quite So Simple*, and a theme: politics did not always turn on black-and-white choices but contained many grays. A liberal Republican, Hatfield found his opposition to the Vietnam War was lifting him into national prominence.

Forever on the move, Hatfield was a hard man to pin down to the lengthy interviews I needed. But in a rather helter-skelter fashion, we got a book finished that quite faithfully mirrored Hatfield's thinking as a progressive Republican and as a force in the party to be reckoned with.

What next? Never bereft of ideas, Arthur proposed that we collaborate on a book about the Broadway theater, and he had a title: *The Playmakers*. It was to be conceived of as a sociological study—exploring the nature of the role of the producer; of the actor; of the director, of the milieu in which they worked. Who were the agents? The lawyers? What was the business side like? We set about profiling the theater as we both then knew it, each from his different perspective. Not without some differences, the collaboration went smoothly enough, and we were both satisfied with the outcome.

As we were feverishly working on the final copy for the book across a table from our editor Evan Thomas, then working for W.W. Norton, my father lay gravely ill in Hartford. When we wound up the work, I rushed home. My mother was downstairs awaiting my arrival. My father lay upstairs in bed. A male nurse was in attendance.

Some years earlier, my father had suffered a stroke in Scotland where he went every other year on business and, not incidentally, to play golf. He played St. Andrews, where he was a member, and through the years, most of the famous Scottish courses. Outside of his family, his friends, and his business, golf, as I have indicated, was his overriding interest. He spent some days in Scotland hospitalized by the stroke and was returned home by plane. Driven by ambulance from New York, he was taken to Hartford Hospital where a disciplined program of rehabilitation enabled him to make a nearly complete recovery.

He supported me in all my endeavors, read my theater columns in the *Tribune*, however foreign the material was to his interests, put money behind me in support of my magazine proposal, and was eager to see the book I was then finishing.

Shortly after his recovery from the stroke, he made one move to bring me, when I was at loose ends, into a business he had in New York as a replacement for its retiring manager. The man interviewed me over a lunch and concluded that I was not right for the job. My father overruled him, but by that time, I too decided that the position was not right for me. It was the only time my father intervened in my professional life, and I suspected that turning to his elder son was due to the realization of a weakening of his own powers brought on by the stroke. It was the one time in my life that I felt my father needed help from me, not me from him. And yet, my course seemed clear. This is how fathers are repaid for a lifetime of generosity.

Now, in August 1969, having spent the night in Fenwick, I climbed the stairs to his room. Gray and frail, he turned his head as I approached. He said one word, "West," his name for me. He took my hand and silently held it for a long moment. Through those clasped hands, a kind of love I had not before experienced with my father passed between us. I left saying I would see him in the morning. He died that night.

The Playmakers was a modest success for W.W. Norton and for Arthur and me. It enabled me to go on to other books, one on off-Broadway, another on Joseph Papp. The creator of Shakespeare in the Park, the winner of a civic battle with the nearly invincible Robert Moses, Papp, taking over what was once the New York Public Library on Lafayette Street, had built a theater complex that expressed his expansionist theatrical and civic ambitions. Several publishers had prodded him to write a book. He had no time for that and came to me suggesting that I take it on. Papp was very much a hero to me. In my newsgathering days, he was invariably forthcoming and direct, not bothering as others did to save his news for the *Times*. I respected him as a courageous, persevering figure in the theater. As I started in on the book, setting out to cover the fast-moving Papp almost on a daily basis, Philip Hamburger, of *The New Yorker*, showed up one day at the Public Theater, assigned to write a profile of Joe. I knew Philip as a friend, and this managed to soften somewhat the competitive jolt I felt. But Hamburger soon left, complaining, "I can't write about this guy. He's moving too fast."

I struggled with my book, too much an admirer of Papp to maintain an objective point of view, too slavishly attached to my day-to-day plan of watching every move of a man of unbounded energy and of prophetic zeal. I finished the book, now appreciating Hamburger's hesitations and realizing with disappointment that I was unable to do justice to a great subject. Papp, who himself with the faintest of apologies had suggested the title, *Enter Joseph Papp*, came away from the book saying, "I didn't know I was so … busy."

Perhaps the most interesting but least satisfactory collaboration I had in theater was with the great acting teacher Stella Adler. An editor I knew who was anxious to put together a book on her acting technique had interested Miss Adler but needed a writer to work with her. My trial interview with Miss Adler took place in the ornately decorated living room of her Fifth Avenue apartment opposite the Metropolitan Museum of Art. Tall and still handsome, her eyes dark with mascara, her lips flaming red, in name and reputation, she was already part of theater legend, and in her late years, she was still flirtatious. With disconcerting intensity, she looked me over from head to toe. Driving home some point of acting technique, she got me out of my chair and onto my feet and put her arms around me drawing me to her. Not ten minutes into our interview, in the middle of her living room, I found myself in a close, silent, prolonged embrace with Miss Adler. Knowing of her renown in younger years for passionate liaisons, I wondered whether she wasn't imposing some sexual test before agreeing to the intimacies of a collaboration. We broke and got down to business. At the end of the interview, I had passed some sort of test.

But I found myself becoming quite jealous during a later working session in her dining room when a handsome, muscular electrician was going about the room on some household repair work, and she glanced up, cast her seductive eyes upon him, and casually said, as if she were merely inquiring about the weather, "Jim, will you marry me?"

I attended her classes, studied her notes, worked with her chastely at the dining room table, and produced a manuscript. She didn't like it at all, and our relationship ended on the telephone. When a book eventually came out by other hands, I noticed it was awfully like my own, in places almost word for word.

In the freelance world, I found it more rewarding financially when I worked with or for others than when I worked for myself. Certainly, it was so when I worked for Jack Dreyfus, once one of the richest men in the United States.

A magazine editor I had worked for, Myra Appleton, was in touch with a *New Yorker* writer who had been offered the chance to work with Dreyfus on a book. When he turned it down, Myra called me. I was passed along to an associate of Jack's to be vetted, then to Dreyfus himself, and was hired.

Jack was a companionable and generous employer. He was a slight man, not tall but good-looking and quick-witted, fond of women and they of him, once married, now divorced. His Jewish background meant little to him in a religious sense, but he was a student of Ouspensky and Gurdjieff. Except on the most formal occasions, he never wore a suit or tie. He came to the office in a blue cashmere sweater and gray trousers. I soon learned that he was rich beyond imagining, living in a penthouse apartment on Madison Avenue opposite the Whitney Museum, his rooms surrounded by gardened terraces with shrubs and roof-grown trees on all sides. He also had a place in Miami, a horse farm in Ocala, a small stone castle on Lake Tahoe, and an island all to himself in Maine, which was a boat ride out of Camden in Penobscot Bay, staffed but rarely visited by him.

Jack traveled among his residences by private jet. His fortune, of course, came from Wall Street where he established the Dreyfus Fund at a time when mutual investment through an ownership share in a managed fund was in its infancy. What he realized through the fund was many times multiplied when he "made the market" for a new stock called Polaroid. Initially, he was intrigued by its 3-D glasses, but what really counted for Jack in the end was the company's success with a camera that developed its own film. And his fortune continued almost spontaneously to grow, which seemed to amaze him more than those around him. One day, as he sat across from me with his feet up in his large corner office in the General Motors Building overlooking Central Park, he shook his head in wonder. "You know," he said, "I acquired quite a bit of land in Texas some time ago. And now they've discovered oil on it." His bafflement over this windfall was genuine. He disclaimed any credit for being farsighted or prescient.

In my work with Jack, I went to Tahoe and the island in Maine, two pieces of real estate that were impressive enough. But it was only many years later, on a visit to Florida, when I saw his horse farm in Ocala that I learned what real wealth in America can bring. Hobeau Farm, as Jack named it, occupies several thousand acres whose soil is enriched with limestone, making it ideal for the care and feeding of horses. This particular county of Florida is home to more breeding farms than any county in Kentucky. The farm is situated in rolling country, interrupted by stands of oak trees, in which the barns and buildings, including a guesthouse, are widely scattered. On a lower level to the west is a first-class one-mile track, one of the few private tracks of such length in the country at the time. Surrounding the property, in which buildings and barns looked spanking new, are fifty miles of four-rail fence painted blue. Two men were detailed full-time to attend to the repair, as well as the repainting, of that fence.

My work with Jack Dreyfus took on quite a different character from the others. I assumed I had been hired to do some form of ghostwriting on a projected book about his experiences with the drug Dilantin, which he had accidentally discovered to be a cure for an endogenous depression he had suffered in mid-career. I soon learned that Jack intended to write the book himself word by word but needed someone in the room with him to organize the work, to bounce ideas off, and to keep him on track. He was willing to accept negative input—the vetoing of ideas he advanced—but not the initiation of new ones by me. I once suggested on paper another title for the book than the one he had in mind, *A Remarkable Medicine Has Been Overlooked*, and, stricken, could hear him across the room, as he glanced at my written suggestion, muttering under his breath, "The impudence, the impudence."

Put together a driven, highly intelligent, compulsive man, accustomed to having his own way, with a crusade, such as Jack had in promoting the drug which he believed had saved his life, and the result is a formidable force to contend with. I was well paid for the work, but my job was all the more trying for being essentially passive, and it was only Jack's unfailing good humor and his acknowledgment that he was difficult that saved us both in our long head-to-head sessions over nearly two years.

I remember being particularly moved by a passage in the book that Jack eventually wrote. He was describing his mental state in the throes of his depression.

> Often I would leave for my [psychiatric] appointment as much as an hour early and kill time by walking. I usually felt cold and would seek the sunny side of the street. After the appointment, if it was daylight, I would walk in Central Park. I would still try to stay in the sun. As the shadows moved across the park, I would walk faster to keep ahead of them.

I understood this search for light and warmth. In my sixtieth year in Fenwick, I was suffering from the onset of rheumatoid arthritis, which made even getting out of a chair a laborious exercise. At the time, Mildred Pond was staying in Fenwick with her sister, our friend Rosemary Murphy. Due to my crippling ailment, she identified me as a candidate for transcendental meditation and came over to the cottage offering to teach me the technique. We met in my upstairs bedroom with its south windows facing the Sound bright with sunlight off the water. She drew up a chair and sat facing me.

"Now, you have to have a mantra, a word of two syllables. Any word will do, but it must be one that you will feel comfortable saying over and over again."

Usually, when challenged this directly, my brain automatically closes down. To my surprise, this time, a word sprang to mind spontaneously. It was a French word, *chaleur*, a word of the required two syllables meaning heat and warmth. To my knowledge, I had never uttered this word before, nor even consciously encountered it, yet now it came as naturally to my ear as if I had known it always. *Chaleur!* In my condition, sunlight and warmth were what I craved. I had transposed the need into a word in a foreign language just as the unknown meditation technique offered by Mildred was now entering my consciousness. The word exactly suited my mood; its use as mantra answered my need. It became my talisman and heralded my recovery.

Some years later, Sandy Otis, a psychoanalyst friend of mine, attributed my case of rheumatoid arthritis to the stress of my confining work with Dreyfus. For the sake of my mental as well as physical health, he cautioned me never to do this sort of work again. The commitment required exhaustive attention, extreme patience, and the kind of neutral objectivity for which, to be sure, the *Tribune* had trained me.

Jack frequently spoke of the important role he felt I had in helping him write the book. Scrupulously fair, he took some guilt upon himself, believing, needlessly, that he had not accorded me enough credit. Jack had a magic touch in everything he did—in finance, in contract bridge and gin rummy, in horse breeding, in golf and tennis. And yet, in his life's all-absorbing passion—getting the medical world and government to accept the value of Dilantin well beyond its limited accepted use—he felt he had come short.

In the early 1980s, on a Sunday morning when my wife was still asleep, the telephone rang. William F. Buckley Jr. was on the line. During college years and afterwards in my many visits to Great Elm, the Buckley family home in Sharon in the northwest corner of Connecticut, to visit his older brother Jim, I had encountered Bill in his younger years. In fact, to be friends with one of the ten Buckley children was to be embraced by the whole family and assumed to be as bright, articulate, engaged, funny, and adventurous as they were. It was a wonderful feeling (politics aside) to be among the Buckleys, as it was the Hepburns in Fenwick, partaking of their brilliance.

My son Christopher, my middle child who had become an accomplished professional photographer, had an even closer relationship with Bill, having signed on as photographer for trans-Atlantic and trans-Pacific voyages with Bill and contributing his work to the inevitable books by Bill that resulted. Starting from a business compact, theirs became a friendship. My relationship with Bill was to become a business one.

My wife protested the early Sunday interruption of his call. The incident was recalled some months later, and Bill's unfailing good manners brought an apology and a promise not to make any further disturbances.

Bill outlined his idea in that telephone call. He proposed a plan to extend the life of an author's book when the publisher declared it out of print. In one of his syndicated columns, he had sketched out the idea. He ran through it for me now. Suppose an author bought up a quantity of his books before his publisher decided to send them to a remainder house. Contractually, publishers are obligated to offer surplus copies to the author first, and the price is right, often little more than a dollar or two. Suppose then the author stored these books in his or her attic or garage. A catalogue would then gather up all these books, list them in a brief description with the author's address, and attach a price the author himself or herself would determine. Such a catalogue would be offered for sale and distributed to libraries and bookstores.

Still in bed, I had to shake off my sleepiness to digest this scheme and respond to Bill's cheerful enthusiasm. Due to my connection with the Authors Guild as editor of its bulletin, Bill thought I could suggest that they take it on. The Guild Council indeed considered the idea favorably while deciding not to undertake it. Bill had an immediate answer to that: "Let's do it ourselves."

Thus the Buckley-Little Catalogue was formed. Bill supplied the brains, the optimism, and the money. I supplied the labor.

"There's nothing as satisfactory as making money in an eleemosynary pursuit," Bill said.

I found space in the Stanford White-designed Cable Building at the corner of Broadway and Houston Street, a short walk from where I lived. In the corner of a loft of an attractive Italian-born woman blouse-maker, whose long cutting table was useful to me for the large mailings I needed to make, I set up a computer and files. Bill located a man to advise us on the computer and data-processing program needed. I found a young woman to key in the detailed information for the catalogue. The Authors Guild Council allowed us to use its list of guild members for a mailing to authors, and we were up and running. Secretly, I always wanted to be an executive. Now I was one—with a makeshift office and a single (part-time) employee. Our debut into the world of publishing, thanks to Bill's name but also to the novelty of the idea, caused a media stir—with coverage in *The New York Times*, the *Wall Street Journal*, and in many other publications. The *Wall Street Journal* piece brought in a flood of individual subscriptions extending over months.

The intricacies of putting the first catalogue to bed were compounded many times by me when I sat down at the computer to perform some final sophisticated data manipulation. The screen abruptly asked me, "Are you sure?" I pressed "Yes" and the entire catalogue was gone—wiped clean. I had never in my life consciously contemplated suicide, but in that horrifying moment when the screen came up blank, I seriously eyed the window of that fourth-floor loft on Houston Street as the only honorable exit. It took some experts Bill knew to restore most of the lost data, and we published on schedule.

We put out the catalogue three years in a row, each year adding more titles. At the third publication, two publishing entrepreneurs called us up with an offer to buy the business. They had a huge warehouse in Westchester, a contract to handle Vatican publications, and far better channels to booksellers and libraries than we did. They offered us enough money to recoup Bill's investment and compensate me for my time. They put out the next year's catalogue, and then, bloated with ambitious offshoots, their company went into bankruptcy and with it the Buckley-Little Catalogue.

Some years later, I went back to the Authors Guild to suggest reviving the idea on the Internet. Coincidentally, they had come to the same conclusion. It was back to the beginning, a return to what Bill originally proposed. The guild tried it for a few years, but it was the difficulty of conceiving a sensible plan of fulfillment that caused the catalogue to founder a second time.

The Buckley-Little Catalogue was an honorable endeavor. Its impact in the world of letters extended further than its brief existence. Writers and their public were made newly conscious of the loss when books went out of print. On a personal level, putting the catalogue together—starting something, running it, making it go—confirmed (belatedly) my father's expectations for me. It was not at quite his own level, to be sure, but it was something.

When, shortly after, I went on to the Theatre Development Fund and, really for the first time since the *Tribune* expired, joined a monthly payroll, I had the same sort of satisfaction starting the TDF newsletter. The newsletter had a ten-year run before the Internet and Web sites overtook the print business and made the newsletter an anomaly.

Chapter 10

Forsaking Fenwick for the South of France

At first, it seemed like an unacceptable hardship to give up a whole summer in Fenwick to visit my parents-in-law at their place in the South of France. As much as I felt a traitor leaving Fenwick, little did I know how seductive life would be in the Midi. One could hardly imagine a more extreme change from life in Fenwick. While my parents-in-law were now a known quantity to me, the strange new ground on which they had taken up residence was not. The baked earth and burning sun of their provincial hillside and the blinding brilliance of the Riviera nightlife they were so fond of in neighboring Cannes were light years removed from our quiet Connecticut existence.

Several years after the war, flush from disposing of several family-owned London properties, my adventure-loving father-in-law, Siegfried Raben, had bought a 110-foot steam yacht which he named *Corax* and on which he intended to sail from Southampton across the channel and down the coasts of France, Spain, and Portugal into the Mediterranean. Yacht ownership, however, was only a strategy on his part.

From England, the *Corax* set forth with its crew of seven. My wife was aboard for the maiden voyage. Remaining behind in New York at my job, I could yet dream of taking part in future voyages to foreign parts. Perhaps the *Corax* would even make it across the Atlantic and into Long Island Sound to amaze Fenwick. It was not to happen. Off Spain, the *Corax* encountered engine trouble and was forced to put in to Santander in the Bay of Biscay for repairs.

The stopover lasted five days, giving owner, passengers, and crew an unintended long look at Santander. Then the *Corax* was on its way again, rounding the Rock of Gibraltar and entering the Mediterranean. Without further incident, she made port in Cannes. There, very shortly, the *Corax* was put on the market, sold, advantageously, and its proceeds used to buy a small but enchanting provincial farmhouse outside the little town of Mouans-Sartoux three miles north of Cannes. Its western windows looked out over a perfumed valley to the hillside town of Grasse. This was Clos d'Amalthée.

My father-in-law found himself in France because he had lost his home in Denmark. The circumstances of his dispossession are rooted in a complicated family history. My father-in-law was born and brought up at Aalholm, which had been in the Raben family since 1725, and before that, since 1375, a royal castle. Aalholm, home of eels, is a great watery fortress on the Baltic coast. It is near the town of Nysted on Lolland, the southernmost island of Denmark facing Germany. Coming upon the castle through the tree-lined drive at dusk, one is awed by the ghostly appearance of the great weathered stone walls of the castle as they rise up darkly in front of one.

In the care of my father-in-law's father, Frederik Christopher Otto, who was foreign minister of Denmark in the first years of the twentieth century, an ugly Victorian addition was made to the castle facing the inner courtyard. In those years, Aalholm saw some of its gayest days, entertaining European royal figures such as Kaiser Wilhelm II of Germany, Edward VII of England, and the King of Sweden.

As the eldest son, my father-in-law was destined to inherit this great property. Instead, it passed to his younger brother, Johann Otto, breaking the succession line from father to eldest son. How this happened is an occasion for competing explanations. One has to do with the marriage contract Siegfried made when he married Pauline. Her determined Anglophilic mother required that the married couple spend half their time in England. By agreeing to this, it was assumed that Siegfried had lost interest in his native country and was not the person to carry on the traditions of Aalholm. In this, there may have been some truth. Another explanation was that Siegfried's capricious mother had favored the younger son and so manipulated the succession that upon the death of Frederik Christopher in 1933, Aalholm passed to Johann Otto.

Dispossessed, my father-in-law became more a part of English life and society than Danish. Summers were spent in Denmark, falls and winters in England, and the children were brought up to be bilingual, speaking English with their mother and Danish with their father. This pattern of life seemed to suit the Rabens. Somehow, the great responsibility of the castle and its lands were not for my talented, lighthearted, and gregarious father-in-law. The nomadic existence suited his temperament better.

The memory of Clos d'Amalthée all these years later induces dizzy delight. The very name makes those moments of the early holiday years in our marriage vivid once again. The Clos stood on the side of a hill, at the end of a steep, winding drive that followed the contours of the hillside. A semicircle of stone steps led up to the walled terrace in front of the house. The dining room was on the left as one entered, a bookcase-lined living room on the right, both with the familiar furniture the Rabens had in London and before that in Denmark. Upstairs, the bedroom windows were ever open, and a breeze would pass through them ruffling the mosquito netting that covered the beds. The house was larger in its depth than its trim, plain facade suggested, and there were enough rooms to accommodate the guests that were always staying, even though there were four in my family—Stuzie, me, and our two children, Caroline and Christopher. At one year old, on our first visit, Christopher spent many of his days lying in perfect contentment nestled on the belly of Edvard, the house's easygoing German shepherd, the two lying drowsily in the noonday heat.

Considerable work by my enterprising parents-in-law had been done on the place before our arrival. At the top of the hill was a large, round cistern fed by a pipe that ran along the ridge and watered the ranked series of narrow walled terraces on which all our vegetables were grown. Everything grew in that rich, watered earth. There were grape arbors, olive trees, almond trees, fig trees, and several varieties of melon for the breakfast table. All this required the care of a full-time gardener and his assistant. In the house were a cook and a maid and a nurse to look after the children. The presence of the staff did not exempt the rest of us from work on the place. My father-in-law had his routines; he was disarmingly well organized. Each morning was spent on a project. One summer, the project was to lay a stone courtyard on the dirt patio at the west side of the house where, beyond the wall, the land dropped off quite steeply into the little town of Mouans-Sartoux well below.

Clos d'Amalthée

From a pile of flat stones, we laid the courtyard piece by piece, evening off each with a level. Straw hats protected us from the burning Côte d'Azure sun. It was hot, tedious work that occupied us many entire mornings. It was harder labor than clipping the hedge in Fenwick. From our squatting positions, as we widened the circle of stones, we eyed the boundary wall, gauging the distance to our goal. On top of the wall were four heads cast in bronze that my father-in-law had sculpted of his children—in order of age, Peter, Anastazia, Charlotte, and Michael. At the rear of the courtyard was a kind of portico where one could sit in the shade and spend the cocktail hour. On its back wall, my father-in-law had painted a large mural depicting the French countryside surrounding the Clos. All this had been done in less than two years.

One summer, we had no sooner arrived than my father-in-law proudly displayed a completed project of significant undertaking—his promised swimming pool. It sat in the garden near the house, not much larger around than a good-sized birdbath and no more than a couple of feet deep. But he had made it with his hands, and it was our swimming pool, perfect for the children to put their toes into, if a little confining for the rest of us.

At the end of morning chores, the rewards were tremendous. There was a large lunch to look forward to and in the afternoon, always an excursion to Cannes to swim, to have dinner, and in the evening to devote time to the tables of the Palm Beach Casino out on the Croisette. The Rabens were a gambling family.

Two carafes of chilled wine, one red, one white, were set out on the dining table for lunch, and one always sampled both. The wine was plain enough, *vin ordinaire* from the town vintner, but it was especially delicious after the sweaty morning work. There were usually a meat course or chicken, a mountainous platter of vegetables fresh from the garden, and, of course, *pommes frites*. It was a large lunch, and a siesta followed before we collected ourselves for the short ride down to Cannes and the day's serious entertainments.

The beach was just below the Croisette running the length of Cannes and was usually crowded with sunbathers in skimpy suits with the occasional serious swimmer. Changing into one's bathing suit on the beach in full view of everyone else in Cannes was somewhat awkward. Nothing in Fenwick beach behavior prepared us for this. It involved wriggling out of one's street clothes, simple though they were, and wriggling into one's bathing suit, a maneuver that was accomplished with some dignity beneath an encircling towel. In time, one learned to be completely impervious to passing cars on the road above and the beach-goers around one. It was only in front of smart hotels that bathhouses existed for private changes of costume. All of this, at the time, under the burning sun and amid the grouping of half-naked, gleaming bodies, seemed quite sexy to me and quintessentially French.

Like Long Island Sound, the Mediterranean was usually quite placid. The children waded in up to their ankles until we persuaded them to be more adventurous, but the main goal of the exercise was simply to cool off. In the late afternoon, the children were sent back to the Clos under the care of their French nurse while we adults searched out a seaside restaurant for the evening meal before setting out for the beckoning rooms of the Palm Beach Casino.

Slacks, espadrilles, and an open quarter-sleeve shirt with a foulard knotted around one's neck constituted a sufficient costume for the casino. Inside, one encountered an infinite variety of exotic dress. For the first few visits, I felt awkward and shy in these foreign surroundings. Who were all these world-weary creatures of many nationalities and disguises arrayed around the playing tables? What was I really doing here among these corseted and lacquered women with their handsome escorts, in this parade of people of indeterminate age and nationality? Night after night, lonely old women could be found fixated on the spinning roulette wheel, looking as if they had not stirred from their seats since the First World War. How very far from Fenwick I was now. And yet—and yet, after only a few more visits, I was to feel completely at home, alarmingly comfortable, in the company of these bizarre people, myself an unexceptional part of the scene.

By the time our second summer at Clos d'Amalthée came, I was fully acclimated—so much so that, leaving our own low stakes *trente et quarante* table, I was emboldened to wander by the high stakes table in the *salle privée*, not of course to play but to observe. That was the summer King Farouk of Egypt, recently married to a seventeen-year-old commoner, was on a gambling honeymoon at Riviera resorts. He came to Cannes on his yacht and settled in of an evening at the no-limit baccarat table. It was possible to watch the play from a discreet distance. I went up to the room with my father-in-law, who could follow the action if not join in it. Farouk was a grand, full-bodied figure flanked on either side by two tall standing Egyptian bodyguards. Seated at Farouk's side was a pretty French girl while his young new wife was safely out of the way on his yacht in Cannes harbor.

Farouk's companions at the baccarat table were themselves household names of the 1950s, particularly to an American. Here were Jack Warner and Darryl Zanuck side by side, deadly rivals in Hollywood but easy companions of the casino. Zanuck shoved his cigar aggressively in front of him and joked with Warner on the side. He may well have been staying with Warner at his villa down the coast at Cap d'Antibes. They were in the constant company of vacuous, decorative women to whom they paid little attention. In these outings, Farouk, Warner, and Zanuck were prepared to win or lose in the thousands of dollars at the turn of a card.

There were other great names wandering the rooms of the casino. One could very nearly rub shoulders with the Duke and Duchess of Windsor, she in a strawberry-decorated dress; Agnelli of Italy who was seeing Pamela Harriman (then Churchill); and Elizabeth Taylor, who at the time was married to Nickie Hilton, left all alone in the bar. These were heady sightings. Time and custom made them seem routine. We all walked the same rooms, breathed the same smoke-filled air, and were catered to indiscriminately by the same croupiers in black tie and jacket. To the croupiers, as I had learned, one tossed a plaque or two after a win—*"pour les personnels."* There was little sign of gratitude on their part.

What mattered more than the company was whether one won or lost. In this respect, casino society was entirely democratic. Disgruntled after an evening of reversals, I made my joke of that summer. Walking away from the casino with Stuzie and Charlotte, I let out a fart and followed it up with the familiar phrase, *"Pour les personnels."* It went down big with the Raben girls.

Side excursions apart from the casino runs were part of those summers. There were picnics in the Gorges du Loup, visits to San Juan Les Pins and Gourdon, lunches and dinners out at the villas of English friends of the Rabens, and afternoons in the swimming pool down the hill from our house at the Duchess of Leinster's. Her naughty daughters swimming around me tried to pull off my bathing trunks.

One evening, we in the family all got dressed up and rode the Grande Corniche down the coast to Monte Carlo for a night of upper-class gambling. As vividly as if it had happened yesterday, I can picture a bloody accident on the road to which we were close witnesses. Two motorcyclists were catching a ride up a hill behind a tour bus when both wobbled, lost balance, and spilled into the road, scraping their unprotected heads raw. We pulled up in horror at the sight. Luckily, two young English doctors were following close behind, also on motorbikes, and stopped to care for the badly injured riders. Relieved of responsibility, we went on to Monte Carlo sobered by the sight and not quite easy at the gambling tables that night.

My father-in-law was fond of planning sporting expeditions. One day, he decided we should go on a fishing trip off Cannes. He located a small fishing boat for charter. The captain promised enormous catches provided one got an early enough start. The early start would also help us avoid such Mediterranean hazards as the mistral. Keeping a weather eye opened for that dreaded ill wind, we set forth at five in the morning on a placid sea equipped for the big catch. We fished the coast back and forth all that morning to make port sunburned and sleepy-eyed at noon with a few fish about as small as minnows.

Next on the schedule was the great chamois shoot on the opening day of the chamois season in the Italian Alps. For weeks, my father-in-law had cultivated the friendship of the local plumber in Mouans-Sartoux who was also, more importantly, *monsieur le president* of the hunting club and a presumed expert on chamois. The night before, to take up accommodations in the hotel, we drove down the coast past Nice and up along the Tinée River to the mountain town of St. Etienne-de-Tinée looking out on the Italian Alps. We had reserved two rooms at the Hotel Issautier, one for

Charlotte and one for my father-in-law and me. Once again, wake-up time was five in the morning so that we could be out on the mountain and in place at the opening hour of the season. M. le President led our party up the mountain trail and positioned each of us in strategic spots to sight the chamois. As an American with no hunting experience, I was placed first at the edge of a clearing about a hundred yards across and was told to keep an eye on an opening in the woods opposite. If not a chamois, M. le President promised, a wild boar was sure to appear. Hugging my gun, I did not take my eyes off the clearing in the woods.

The rest of the party went on up higher. Of course, no wild boar crossed the sights of my gun, let alone a chamois. But in this respect, I was not alone. M. le President was the only one in our party even to sight a chamois that day. He spent some time explaining to the rest of us why he missed his shot. In fact, at the appointed hour of the opening of the season, one could hear guns popping all over the mountainside. By the time the members of our party were in place, the chamois had scampered several mountain ranges distant.

For my father-in-law, the success of these sporting ventures was more frequently measured in the zeal of his preparations and in the fervor of his expectations than in the outcome. But this indeed was true of many aspects of his life: the enthusiasm was childlike and eager; the result often fell short of the goal. Somehow, the end result didn't matter all that much. It was the doing that counted, and his irrepressible spirits overrode any disappointment.

Abandoning the hunting, I went up the back of a mountain ridge for a better view of the Bec de Marseille, the most prominent peak in sight. The path up the ridge was hardly a yard wide. I began to question the wisdom of this adventure. When I attempted to turn around on that ribbon of a path and retrace my steps, I panicked. The falloff to the right into dense forest was so precipitous that I looked down tremblingly on the tops of trees. On the left was a loose shale escarpment pitching almost straight down hundreds of yards. I was frozen into complete immobility and could neither turn nor take a step. My father-in-law, some distance below, realized my predicament and called up to talk me down. I eventually made my uncertain descent on the seat of my pants.

As a child, one climbs the tall tree almost in anticipation of a fall. More often, one reaches the high place before experiencing the danger. On that mountain ridge, I realized too late that one small misstep would have been a fatal dive.

While the attraction to danger is mysterious, escape from danger is not exhilarating, as one might expect, but often a letdown. Once, in Mexico, I found myself in a situation of danger compounded by the near impossibility of escape. When it was all over, I was left only with flattened emotion.

We were traveling in Mexico with two close friends from Princeton, Sandy Otis, a Jungian analyst, and his Norwegian-born wife, Grete, my wife's oldest friend in America. We were staying with their friends, Percy and Nancy Wood, at their beach house in Acumal in Quintana Roo on the Caribbean. They were to become our friends also. One day, Percy suggested a swimming expedition and picnic at a remote beach about ten miles down the coast from their house. From the road, where we parked the car, a narrow path a quarter of a mile long led through the brush to the beach. Percy, a psychiatrist colleague of Sandy's, had a sense of the dramatic.

"Now, I want to warn you," Percy began soberly, "the *quatre nores* snake is sometimes to be found in this area. It is extremely dangerous. The poison of its bite can result in instantaneous death. In fact, I have heard of a brave Mexican who was bitten on the arm by the snake while on horseback. Instantly, to save his life, he took out his machete and hacked his arm off."

After this cheerful story, we all fell silent on our walk through the underbrush. Happily, we reached the beach without having encountered the *quatre nores* snake. The path opened out into a sandy shore ringed by palm trees. In a clearing were some rough wooden picnic tables and benches. Not a soul was in sight. The sandy beach, at the head of a narrow inlet leading out to the sea, was bordered on one side by an impenetrable wall of rocks and on the other by a sheer cliff rising from the water's edge.

Before any of us knew it, Sandy was in swimming. Far out in the inlet, as it met the sea, he could be heard calling for help. A swift undercurrent had taken him out of the inlet to open water, and now, he couldn't get back. He was caught in the current. Foolishly, I set out to swim after him, not really thinking he could be in too much trouble. A minute or so passed, and I realized I too was moving out of the inlet much faster than my own capacity to swim. When I was within fifty yards of my friend, I turned around to test the current taking me out. I was caught too. I swam hard towards shore and did not move on the land.

Now my only thought was to try to regain ground myself. There was no way I could rescue Sandy. A hundred yards from me, towards shore, a rock was awash in the rushing water. If I could get to that island rock, I could cling to it and rest. Inching my way to the rock, I reached it at last, scraping my legs bloody as I flattened my body against it. Twice, the water rushing over the rock threatened to break my hold.

By this time, those on shore had been alerted. Percy and Grete ran out along the cliff and called to us, Grete distraught at realizing the full extent of Sandy's predicament. From his high perch above me, Percy gave instructions in a calm voice. On the rock, I was not far from the shore, but there was no landing place at the foot of that cliff rising sheer from the water. Percy got the branch of a tree to hold down to me. Reaching the shore from the rock more easily than I expected, I grabbed hold of the branch, and they lifted me up along the cliff onto the bank. Next, it was Sandy's turn. He followed my route to the rock, rested there, and came into the shore, but getting up along that rocky cliff caused a new terror in him. Wearing no bathing suit, he was in an agony of fear that on that jagged cliff, an essential part of his anatomy would be torn away.

Sandy made it safely up to the bank in one piece. At the picnic table, rejoining the group, he sat apart, behind the rest of us, having been roundly scolded for causing everyone such worry, endangering his own life, and risking another's as well. Years later, Percy remembered my wife saying, "Sandy, you almost spoiled our picnic." Soon enough, he was his old self, advising me not to cover my bloody legs in town; the Mexicans would love the sight.

As for Clos d'Amalthée, in idle, fanciful moments, we children (including me) imagined that the Clos would one day pass to us. Endless summers in the South of France were foreseen stretching before us. It was too perfect a dream to come true. The Rabens gave up the Clos and moved again, this time to Wicklow in Ireland and a house on the water equivalent in size and charm to the Clos. Soon, they had new gardens flourishing under their care.

Chapter 11

"Suffer the Little Children"

In the 1950s, my family—Stuzie, the three children, and Nurse—had the cottage pretty much to ourselves. Nurse took to Fenwick as she took to New York because that was where the family was. She was part of it. Stuzie's childhood nurse in England and Denmark had been "Nurse" not a "nanny" because she had been trained at Norland, the respected school for children's nurses in England. She merited the distinguishing title.

One summer, my mother invited Nurse, then in her mid-seventies, to come up to their cottage, where meals would be cooked for her, for a rest. To legitimatize the vacation in her own mind, Nurse brought along our third child, Suzanne, then about three.

One likes to think all one's children are exceptional. Suzanne was so from birth, beginning with the place and circumstances of that event. She was born in Sydenham Hospital, a city hospital in Harlem. (My friend Dick Dougherty, then Deputy Commissioner of Hospitals, recommended Sydenham, saying that city hospitals were cleaner than private hospitals.) A prominent patient in the hospital at the time, on the same floor as my wife, was the Harlem gangster Ellsworth "Bumpy" Johnson, recovering from shooting wounds. A headline name in the newspapers, he was widely known for running the numbers racket in Harlem as well as for other illegal activity. In that long night of waiting I sat with several police officers who were there to provide protection to Johnson while on city property. He was a material witness in his own shooting but had refused to testify against his assailant. I caught glimpses of him walking the hall and making covert telephone calls. To a nervously waiting father, his mysterious comings and goings were almost as diverting as the prospect of the event to come. Early that Sunday morning of June 22, 1952, having recovered enough to be discharged, Johnson dressed and slipped out into a darkened Harlem where, presumably, someone wishing him harm might be waiting to finish the job. The cops were through with him after he walked out the door. An hour or so after Bumpy Johnson's departure, Suzanne came into the world. I wondered if that was a good pairing—my newborn child and Bumpy Johnson.

There was a more felicitous pairing. Suzanne was born on Nurse's birthday, creating a special bond between them. Together, they went on up the beach to my parents' cottage for a three-week stay while the rest of us remained behind in the old cottage.

In the psychological history of our family, this seemingly benign move may have had unintended consequences. In retrospect, it raised many questions. Did the child see herself as exiled and punished by being removed from the center family? It was just a short stretch of beach away, and the two houses were within eyesight of each other, but to a child, space and time are indeterminate. Did this apparently inexplicable exile cause her in later years to feel excluded from the family? Or, rather, was it the beginning of her independent spirit? Perhaps the concern was more in the mind of Stuzie because it seemed to repeat the mistakes of her own upbringing. So often in her own childhood, she was separated from her socially busy parents in London, and she was left in the care of a grandmother in the Wiltshire countryside—in this case, an unsympathetic and disagreeable grandmother who anyway favored her older brother over her. Again and again, whenever some memory of the past was reawakened and this disturbing event of Suzanne's childhood seemed to reassert itself, Stuzie's own childhood pain resurfaced and she would berate herself for having allowed that brief summer's separation from her then very young daughter.

All three children made Fenwick friendships that have survived to the present day. Suzanne put her lonely visit to her grandparents behind her to form, at the age of five, a romantic attachment to Duggie Reigeluth, which involved an early exchange of rings. He was but one member of a family that had matching age and gender counterparts to our three children. In fact, another Fenwick family, as it happened, was so fortunately arranged as to provide companions for each of them.

Since we lived next door to Pooh Brainard, Caroline was within shouting distance of her friend, and the two were able to plan their days before breakfast from second-story bedroom windows. Christopher had his own companions. Upon our arrival each summer, the friends would gather around as the bicycles were unpacked and the friendships would resume seamlessly where they had left off the summer before.

On one bright sunny morning, Nurse dressed the children in their tidiest best summer clothes, washed and scrubbed their faces, and slicked back their hair. A professional photographer was coming to take their pictures. They were to pose on the lawn in front of my parents' cottage. The camera caught them in their uncomfortable perfection. Caroline, aged nine, is skipping toward the photographer in a spotlessly white muslin summer dress, white socks, and buckled shoes. Blonde Christopher, three years younger, in a white shirt and grey shorts, is kneeling on the grass. And Suzanne, three years younger than her brother, is shown in profile with a toothy smile.

I don't know why these photographs of our lovely threesome have always made me sad. Perhaps they are too perfect-looking, too obedient-seeming, too altered from their carefree summer selves. Were they being pushed into living up to some Nurse-imposed model of perfection? Did I want to roughen up those pristine images and put them on a better footing with their Fenwick companions?

As soon as our first child, Caroline, was born, Nurse had packed her belongings in England and sailed for New York, asking nothing but to be here, serve Stuzie, and care for the new baby. We paid her a ridiculously small wage. In the limited two-bedroom apartment we first occupied at 165 East Sixtieth Street, where eventually the three children slept together in the back bedroom, she took what was available—a bed made up in the dinette off the kitchen. She never complained, living in that tight little apartment in the noisy middle of Manhattan so far removed from the life she was used to in the sedate streets of Belgravia.

In addition to the care of the children, she usually prepared our meals and pushed the baby carriage to the park. When no park trip was scheduled, the carriage went out onto the balcony off our living room facing the loading platforms of Bloomingdale's. Five stories above noisy Sixtieth Street, yet undisturbed by all the traffic that flowed off the Queensboro Bridge and the rattle of the Third Avenue El, the baby slept soundly until the sun went down behind the high west wall of Bloomingdale's and carriage and baby would be lifted back indoors.

In Fenwick, Nurse lent a veneer of distinction to the small family. No one else in Fenwick had an English nurse—servants, yes, but no English nurse. In those days, the back of our cottage, like those of all the others, was honeycombed with small rooms for the cook, maid, and nurse in the family.

As soon as Nurse arrived to join the family, our life became unimaginable without her. She was an inseparable part of Fenwick summers. A dignified, gentle woman, she had defined standards that were instantly recognized and respected by anyone with whom she came into contact. Once, when she was departing by ship for England for a holiday with the children, I impulsively kissed her good-bye. She was so taken aback that I never attempted it again. People of my parents' generation, accustomed as they were to dealing with servants, and sometimes with not altogether satisfactory servants, made something of a fuss over Nurse, and no one more so than my mother.

In the summer of 1962, Nurse was too ill to come to Fenwick. She remained behind in New York, staying with me at the apartment in the hot months. By this time, we had moved one floor down in our little building opposite Bloomingdale's to an apartment double the size of our first New York home on the fifth floor. This gave Nurse a room of her own. It was a tiny room at the back, and because of the breathlessness that resulted from her illness, she moved to the larger, airier bedroom that was shared by our two daughters, Caroline and Suzanne, then sixteen and ten years old. She lay there in the heat, becoming weaker and weaker, until finally, I summoned Stuzie from Fenwick. She returned to New York, leaving the children to care for themselves, and we saw Nurse into St. Luke's Hospital. In three days, she died at the age of eighty—almost her entire life having been spent in the love and care of the children of one family.

We called Fenwick and instructed the children to take the train to New York. A piece of our little family had been torn away. There was no way to tell them on the telephone. We met them at Penn Station and walked them to the car. Suzanne, Caroline, and Stuzie got in the back. Christopher sat beside me on the front seat. Before starting out, we told them Nurse, their Nurnie, had died. From the back seat, Caroline said, "I knew it. I knew it. I knew that was why you called." Suzanne and Christopher were silent. Sitting beside me in the front seat, Christopher, in shorts and polo shirt, was blonde, slight, and small. He kept very still. We sat there in silence. In a minute, his face twisted, and he collapsed into sobs. And then we were all of us in tears. We had lost the one person in all of our lives who gave unqualified love. Suzanne was born on her seventieth birthday. The children had never known anyone else. Hers was the first death in the family.

Nurse lies in Cedar Cemetery at Saybrook Point. Only the family gathered around for the interment. Standing somewhat apart, our friend Dick Hepburn, a surprise mourner, kept a respectful distance, silent throughout the ceremony. At the head of the plot, her stone would read, "Suffer little children to come unto me."

Having Nurse for all those years of child-rearing allowed Stuzie (and me) a certain freedom. In the 1950s, when the two oldest children were in school, Stuzie got a job in a bookstore on Lexington Avenue five blocks from where we then lived. A reader herself, she was a successful salesperson, often being able out of her own reading to match the customer with a suitable book. During this period, particularly, her reading was so constant a part of her routine that even today, the children recall it and complain that in their childhood, her head was always in a book to the point of neglecting them.

Stuzie worked crossword puzzles, double crostics, and cryptograms routinely and later devised such puzzles herself professionally for *Actors' Equity* magazine and, under a different name, for *AFTRA* (American Federation of Television and Radio Artists) magazine, inking out the grids herself.

She studied people who entered the bookstore and could read character traits in chance remarks. She listened in on conversations on the street, drawing out of them daily dramas that probably existed more in her imagination than in reality. She noted the clothes people wore, filed away odd expressions, and began to write plays.

Stuzie brought her writing projects to Fenwick and set up her typewriter on a table in the window of our bedroom. Passersby on the waterfront path in front of our cottage would hear the clacking of the keys. Dick Hepburn, a fellow playwright, could be an interrupting visitor from time to time. He brought the diversion of discussing his own dramatic projects and his vivid character sketches of Old Saybrook personalities who eventually would show up as characters in his plays. Dick would usually be in the midst of tracking some potential producer or urging a play of his on some actress he wanted to interest, but the projects rarely reached fruition.

A favorite niece of Dick's, Katharine Houghton, the daughter of Dick's sister Marion and her husband, Ellsworth Grant, was an actress and also a playwright. She was more a visitor than a summertime resident, staying with her parents two cottages east of us on the seafront. Stuzie once showed a script of hers to Kathy and got back such a disagreeably negative reaction that my own appreciation of Kathy's work was thereafter in our house considered unacceptable.

Playwriting, writing dialogue, and dramatizing behavioral traits in people came naturally to Stuzie. She had two of her dramatic pieces produced. One was a musical of the 1970s performed at Joseph Papp's Public Theater entitled *Don't Fail Your Lovin' Daddy, Lily Plum*. The other was a comedy, *The Double Game*, produced by Arthur Cantor at the off-Broadway Perry Street Theater.

Underlying the writing that surfaced, as it does for most writers, was an iceberg of tries. In the late 1980s, she wrote *The Grandparents' Book: The Joys and Frustrations of Coping with Your Offspring's Offspring*, which was illustrated brilliantly by Roy McKie. She insisted that my name join hers in authorship, but it was really her work. Her next project was the translation and editing of the travel writings of Hans Christian Andersen who had once been a tutor to her Danish grandfather. It was published by Green Integer Press in 1999. That same year, her translation of Andersen's accounts of his boyhood won a translation prize from the American Scandinavian Foundation.

Later still, in her seventies and eighties, Stuzie, among other projects, is laboring long over a novel-length work entitled *Meet the In-laws* which deals with the interrelationships of three families of uncommon quirkiness observed through the eyes of two observant and inquisitive cleaning women.

Where, I wondered, did all this creative energy and tumult of effort come from? Partly, I thought, it came from a feeling of alienation from the culture in which she found herself: both a rebellion and an attempt at understanding, an escape into a world of her own making and at the same time, an engagement. After initial caution, Stuzie had been totally accepted by the wives of my friends. All of them had gone to college, many of them to the same college at the same time, creating exclusive bonds among them. She had never had any formal education and felt the discrepancy keenly. Did she hope that her work would right the balance? No matter the reason, her writing has continued as part of her life throughout the years.

Chapter 12

Newcomers Arriving

"A Victorian Commune" was how Marion Grant characterized Fenwick. Few of us had thought as seriously about the place as she had. No one else had so successfully condensed the essence of Fenwick into words. As a Hepburn, she had spent summers in Fenwick since childhood, and now, in a cottage of her own, she had a family of three children who were Fenwick born and bred and embodied the strong sense of independence that marked every Hepburn. Handsome and bold of feature, they were clear descendants of their Hepburn grandparents. Marion herself, in her marriage and in the life she and her husband Ellsworth adopted, had broken away and chosen a more conventional style. This brought about the occasional derision of her provocative brother Dick.

Marion and her husband were both writers and dreamers, but their dreams had a utilitarian side. Their many projects arose out of their acceptance of the existing society whereas the older Hepburns had rejected it, with their radical strategies for asserting women's rights, by advocating birth control and fighting "social" disease. The politics that supported these then unpopular ideas were not the politics of Marion and her husband. Practical idealists, they accepted the community as it was and worked within the community for its betterment. Their view of Fenwick was broad enough also to encompass the town of Old Saybrook, of which

Fenwick, with its borough form of government, was a part. Except for the borough officers, few of us had contact with the town, except to pass through, go to the movies, sit at Miss James's ice-cream counter, and shop at Faulk's Store or Ingram's Fish Market. For Marion and Ellsworth, a sense of civic responsibility was strong, resulting in their considerable contributions to town life—promoting the library, preserving park land, and other projects.

Marion's richly researched history of Fenwick, *The Fenwick Story*, held a mirror up to who we were and who we are. As a written record enlarges one's sense of a place and time, *The Fenwick Story*, for all of us, deepened the experience of being a living community on that small peninsula bounded by the river and the Sound, summer after summer. An opening section of the book traced the history of the land in colonial times. In later sections, she took inventory of the indigenous trees, flowers, birds, and fishes that abound in the area. Every athletic event was listed, every Fenwick trophy winner named.

But the heart and core of the book are the biographies of all the Fenwick families, arranged cottage by cottage, up one row and down another. This was a careful accounting. She had to cajole and badger each of us to contribute the particulars of our several stories. She worked relentlessly, and the result was a detailed genealogical and biographical profile of each Fenwick family. Threaded through these accounts were the cross-lines of relationship between families, descending from the Bulkeley, Brainard, Davis, and Goodwin patriarchs.

Line drawings of each cottage accompanied each account. The cottages are identified by the families who occupied them, the families by the cottages. Marion meticulously recorded building dates and listed the original and previous owners in sequence. Most cottages sprang up in the same period, the late years of the nineteenth century, shingled Victorian-style structures with paneled tongue-and-groove walls and ceilings. They vary in size and pretension. The shorefront cottages on the front line tend to be rather grand and imposing, with wide porches and pillars and gabled roofs. Our own cottage was moderate in size, not on the grand scale, but not a bungalow either, with its six bedrooms, dining room, large kitchen, and comfortably sized living room. In Fenwick houses, life is lived on the porches. We were no exception to this rule. Proud of his own large west porch, which he called "the best porch in Fenwick," my father was smart enough not to broadcast this boast beyond our household.

My father, with rolled-up sleeves, used to trim the privet hedge along the east edge of our cottage with hand shears. The task was lightened in my day by the use of electrical clippers, but it was still a full morning's work. There were no fences around Fenwick properties. From the earliest years, it was an acceptable practice to cut across anyone's lawn getting from one part of Fenwick to another.

A Victorian commune, Marion called it. It was Victorian partly because of the architecture, partly because its preserved customs recalled the time of its founding. It was a commune because property lines were obscured and families had a way of melding. Children away from their immediate homes were looked after in other homes as if they belonged. Very often they did, by relationship. Property lines were ignored. Games of kick-the-can took place on anyone's front lawn or backyard. Hide-and-seek ranged around the corners and within the latticed laundry-yards of anyone's cottage. Fenwick was small enough, cohesive enough in its population, and similar enough in its social values and principles to act as the home of one large extended family. Part of this was due, too, to the tangled blood lines among Fenwick families. Cousins were everywhere. Until the late 1950s, Fenwick was largely simply the summer extension of the lives of a small and prosperous circle of prominent, interrelated Hartford families. This would change in the 1960s.

It would change because of outsiders buying in, and it would change because of a cohort of four friends who discovered Fenwick and brought their large families to summer here, first by renting cottages for part of the summer, eventually by buying cottages of their own and settling in. The old families were not yet ready to retreat and be replaced by new blood, but the new families—the Millards, the Rehms, the Chmiels, and the Barretts—brought some sharp contrasts, like their Catholicism, for one thing, against the prevailing Episcopalianism. Their large families followed. Fenwick ostensibly was divided into two large families—on the one hand, the new families whose shared values brought them together into one family, and on the other, the older Fenwick families joined by relatedness and custom.

Two of the four new family patriarchs, Millard and Rehm, graduates of Holy Cross, were bound together by college ties. They traveled together in Fenwick. The four were socially close, always making up an annual threesome or foursome in the Labor Day Tournament. Between two of the families, in time, there was even intermarriage as when a Rehm married a Millard. The houses of both families were added to in order to accommodate the increase in numbers as the children married and began families of their own. These building additions were ones that perhaps our zoning regulations did not strictly encourage. Fenwick expanded. The new interweaving of family ties was no longer Hartford, no longer Protestant. It was friendly and conformist, but a new culture.

It was ironic to find living within the limited boundaries of this narrow little community, one family, the Hepburns, renowned for their advocacy of birth control and, as a result, their strong antipathy to Catholicism, and the four new growing Catholic families stretching to new limits the population capacities of Fenwick.

I recalled the Buckley family in Sharon, Connecticut, the family that produced a United States Senator and U.S. Court of Appeals Judge in James L. Buckley and the writer, novelist, editor, debater, lecturer, sailor, and founder of *National Review* in William F. Buckley Jr. There were ten children, the eldest of whom had ten children of her own. My close friend in the family, Jim, was to have six. Through the Buckleys, I became conscious of the inherent strength of large Catholic families, of the ways they support each other and rally to the cause of one of their members, of their use of numbers to extend their influence into the community, and of their apparent absence of youthful rebellion or deviation from the parents' philosophy, political or social. In large families, the whole is greater than the sum of its parts. Intellectually, the Buckley family coalesced around a core of conservative principles and religious beliefs which propelled them into national life. Like the Kennedys in politics, they have had an impact on our public life, in large part responsible for a shift towards conservativism in American thinking.

The new families had an obvious impact on Fenwick, too—the enlargement of the borough. First-generation Fenwick families were themselves large. Five or more children was more or less the norm (even in the Hepburn family there were six), and the cottages were of a size to accommodate them. But in their children, the birth rate was lowered to more moderate levels. Where there had been families with five or six children, there were now families with two or three—until the new large families came to Fenwick and made numbers the controlling influence on the place.

What do numbers have to do with the character of Fenwick? At first, and during the early years of the new families, the community was split between the old and the new. Inevitably, suspicion was attached to the newcomers. Would they by virtue of their numbers, wealth, and position edge out the old ruling order of Fenwick and displace the descendents of the founding families? This was the unexpressed fear. They weren't "us." Rather, they came respectful of the Fenwick they found and did not presume to seek for themselves special advantage or the positions of power but instead allied themselves with and supported those who held power and position by long custom. They had no candidate to put up for warden. They deferred tactfully to those who, so to speak, spoke for Fenwick. On the great occasions, such as the Fourth of July, Labor Day, and, post-season, Columbus Day in October, when almost everyone returned to Fenwick for the long weekend and the Long Ball Contest, the whole community came together. Athletically, the two Fenwicks met.

With golf ascendant, the Labor Day Tournament and the winning of the Morgan Cup became the chief athletic goal of every male Fenwick golfer. Playing for the trophy was the climactic event of the summer. To enter the winner's circle of Morgan Cup holders was the ultimate Fenwick achievement. Possession of the cup bound one to the mystical past of Fenwick, in the words of the Fenwick hymn, "to the presence of those dear saints gone before."

Edith Gengras

Morgan Cup winners 1999

The new families grasped the meaning of the Morgan Cup. They embraced the central emblem of Fenwick life. On their own initiative, they were to surround the trophy with a new aura, enhancing and embellishing its symbolism in their own way. The spoils to the winner were grandly multiplied: an engraved Tiffany crystal disc for the winner to keep on his mantle and a poster-size reproduction of the Morgan Cup blown up for the wall. Besides the winner's name in calligraphic script, a small line-cut of his cottage occupied a corner of the poster. (In my own case, when I won in 1988 and a second time in 1995 a small error appeared on the grand Morgan Cup poster: my brother's cottage was reproduced instead of my own.) All this was in addition to the green coat with its gold-threaded representation of the cup that was ceremoniously draped over the shoulders of the winner by the previous year's cup holder. The hundred-year-old trophy acquired a new shine.

Fenwick gained new vitality and luster from the presence of the new families. Their numbers alone assured them full participation in Fenwick life in every field of activity, beginning with beach life at the pier, the play class, and organized sports. Mutual suspicion subsided—the old-timers for the newcomers, the newcomers for the old-timers. Yet there existed a residue of uneasiness, particularly on the old Hartford-based Fenwick side. Even our proud Aetna Life inheritance meant little to the newcomers.

Normally, the give and take of Fenwick life has an equalizing effect. When everyone is on vacation time, individual importance evens out. There goes just another golfer, another tennis player, another Morgan Cup winner or hopeful, another jogger down the dirt roads of Fenwick. But on one occasion, their actual roles in life—their non-Fenwick importance—came into clearer focus, and I saw them all in a new light, assembled, waiting, on the lawn in front of my cottage to hear a campaign pitch from my good friend Jim Buckley. Defeated in New York by Daniel Patrick Moynihan for reelection as senator in 1980, he had come into Connecticut (actually his home state) to run for the United States Senate there.

I assumed some monetary and other support could be found in Fenwick for his candidacy. In the new blood in Fenwick, Catholic and Republican, he could not have discovered a more congenial constituency. I persuaded him to stop off one late August afternoon after an exhausting swing through southern Connecticut to appear before the Fenwick group I managed to assemble. Old Fenwick, as it happened, was not well represented at this gathering. The new families were—their Catholicism and their Republicanism responding to those of the candidate.

As Jim arrived with his wife, Ann, hot and dusty from the campaign trail, his coat slung over his arm, I tried to usher him directly into the house past the waiting guests so that he could go upstairs to change and freshen up. One persistent guest, a dyed-in-the-wool conservative, kept plucking at his sleeve, figuratively speaking, detaining him with questions and pressing his own opinions. I finally freed the candidate to make his brief escape.

We reassembled, he and I, on the front porch. To our backs, beyond the porch railing was the sparkling blue Sound. It was a sunny late afternoon. The hedge bordering the east lawn was freshly clipped for the occasion. One could have run a string along its flat top from one end to the other without a ripple.

After my introduction, Jim made a graceful disclaimer disengaging me from his politics. Friends though we were, he acknowledged that we probably disagreed on most substantive political points. After his talk, I introduced him around. I could see these important prospective donors on the lawn, expectant, standing on one foot and then the other, waiting for an introduction to be performed, wary I thought of being slighted. Most of them were CEOs, and now it was that persona rather than their relaxed Fenwick selves that came to the fore. They were no longer quite my easygoing Fenwick neighbors.

It was an odd moment for me. I had a cottage in Fenwick, a base. I had an old friend in politics. I had these new friends who could help. I was pleased by the accident of being able to bring the two together, yet I was part of neither the one nor the other. I had neither the politics of my friend, shared as it was by this Fenwick group, nor, even had I wanted to participate, the means they had to help.

On this occasion, I was especially conscious of my anomalous position. My ownership of the cottage in Fenwick was due not to my own efforts but to the good fortune of having had an industrious and successful father. I could be satisfied that he would have stood comfortably among these new Fenwick friends and would have happily endorsed the politics of my friend Jim. In retrospect, that seemed to confer a certain legitimacy on my ambiguous role. I was a stand-in for old Fenwick. But they were the new coming-on Fenwick. I could not then acknowledge or see that it would be they who would account for the regeneration of Fenwick, that they, in their time, would somehow be the heirs to the first families, not yet quite displacing them, but running in tandem with them, shaping the new Fenwick, all the while adhering to, indeed embracing, all its old traditions.

Chapter 13

Through the Sixties

The red Honda motorcycle on its kickstand waits by the front walk at the hedge. The weekend is over. With laundry cord, Christopher has strapped down a knapsack on the rear passenger seat. He puts on his leather jacket with *Triumph* stitched across the back. On his throttle hand, he slips the handball glove with the tips of the fingers cut off. He pauses a moment before fitting the helmet with its protective face shield on his head, half waiting for the good-bye kiss, not quite ready to initiate it himself. We kiss him, his mother and I. The helmet goes on. He kicks the Honda into gear, rolls across the lawn, steadying the motorcycle with his toes, and goes through the narrow opening in the hedge onto the road. Obedient to the traffic sign, he pauses at the corner, then disappears behind a neighbor's hedge. Moving up on the throttle, he is away once more.

   Wasn't it only moments ago that we were sending him off on a two-wheeler down the front walk, the two parents running alongside hoping he could make it past the Brainard cottage next door before falling off? Fenwick, as all parents knew, was a great learning ground for children, where the first swimming strokes were taken, the first swings of the golf club and tennis racquet, the first competitive encounters with other children at group sports. They learned how to be sociable and how to be good sports. Now new games were being played.

Away in boarding school at Hotchkiss in Lakeville, Connecticut, Christopher was developing his interest in photography, the inquiring eye behind the lens that was to lead to his ultimate career. He was single-minded in this pursuit. A friend of mine, a Harvard classicist, once said he believed it didn't much matter what you did in life. What did matter was sticking to the work one chose. In years to come, I admired in Christopher the undeviating line of his interest while at the same time pondering, against my friend's wise words, the wavering line of my own professional life.

At his boarding school, Christopher had a strong champion in George Stone, a mathematics teacher whom I had known in college. George was the younger brother of Lou, with whom I had shared that grand flat in Upper Grosvenor Street in London during the war and who had blessed my wartime engagement to Stuzie. While these ties existed between the Stones and the Littles, the bond between George and Christopher in school had a life of its own. George had a caustic sense of humor that was intimidating to defenseless students. Christopher was not among those.

At Hotchkiss, George allowed himself an unexpected, curiously out-of-character sentimentality over Christopher, as if, for the time being, for the duration of his term at Hotchkiss, and in the cloistered atmosphere of the school, he was the child George and his wife, Jodie, never had.

The Stones now decided that in recognition of the level of his competency in photography, he deserved the best equipment, and they proposed that we go in with them in buying it—a graduation present to be enjoyed in advance: a top-of-the-line Nikon, with all the accessories and extra lenses.

In the summer before his senior year at school, Christopher's spirits were high. He was one of four members of his class picked to take part in the GO (Greater Opportunity) Program. He would be in charge of a group of inner-city boys who would come to the Hotchkiss campus in the summer to participate in a program of sports, recreation, and lessons, making use in the off-season of that school's unrivaled facilities. It was an honor to have been chosen, and he was proud. The headmaster wrote each of the four picked to lead the program to share his high hopes "for a successful outcome of the coming summer." Christopher's reaction to these fine words was predictably irreverent. "It sounds like an advertising pamphlet for Camp Peachykeen on Lower Bassethound Bay!"

In fact, it was far from being an easy summer for Christopher. Taking a weekend off in the middle of the GO Program to be with us in Fenwick, Christopher came back taller than last time, we noticed, and more serious. But it was his way to dispel the sober mood with a joke or two, often one on himself. He quoted a boy from Bedford-Stuyvesant in Brooklyn: "Back where I come from, the white boy rides in the back of the bus."

As proctor, besides English classes and math tutorials, Christopher was responsible for basketball, volleyball, and baseball—his authority not resting on his own abilities at these games but rather on what powers of persuasion he was able to summon to keep his teams motivated. He met with sullen resistance from a tall, powerfully built boy named Zulu. Basketball suffered. His team slipped to the bottom of the league. After a bad game, Christopher called after Zulu, but he refused to stop. He overtook Zulu but Zulu refused to speak to him. "All right," Christopher said, "I'm going to take you to Father Kern."

Father Kern was the head of the GO Program, but he declined to take Christopher's part in the dispute. Christopher decided to make one more try with Zulu. He would compromise and meet him halfway. Zulu began speaking to Christopher again. After the next game, Christopher called the team together. "Zulu and I," he told them, "have come to an agreement."

The effect on the team was instantaneous. They won that game. The team rose to the top of the league in basketball and to second place in volleyball and baseball.

Out of that summer came a memento—a photograph he had taken of a lanky African-American boy whose long thin arm shot upward with fingers extended tipping a basketball into the basket. The boy was Zulu. Christopher had signed the photograph and given it to his mother and father. "This is my favorite picture, and it is for you, Papa & Mum. Christmas 1968. All love, Christopher."

Coinciding with Christopher's return to Fenwick from the GO Program was an angry telephone call from his schoolmaster George Stone. I took the call and listened, abashed, to George's complaint. He had brokered that loan of a friend's Honda motorcycle to Christopher and felt responsible. Now, he claimed, Christopher had returned it after six weeks of use without seeing that it was properly serviced. George, Christopher's strong champion, had turned. "I'd like to burn that kid's tail. I'd like to skin him alive." This abrupt change of attitude from the admiring George for whom Christopher could do no wrong to the enraged George who could hardly contain his anger at him shocked and silenced me. Even if the charges were true, could an inadequately serviced Honda have provoked such an eruption of irritation and anger?

Shortly after the burning telephone call, Christopher arrived at the cottage by car from school in Lakeville, having been driven home by a fellow proctor in the program. A mountain of camera gear was soon piling up in the living room—the splicer, the rewinds, the Nikon carrying case with the extra lenses, the light stands, reflectors, and tripods. I then reported as calmly as I could the call from George Stone. Not altogether surprised, Christopher smiled when he heard the story. "Mr. Stone has been a little ticked off at me lately. I think I know why." He promised to call the owner of the Honda. The motorcycle, he said, had been serviced properly, and he had returned it in good condition. And he would call Mr. Stone.

With his mother, Christopher had discussed a coolness George Stone had shown towards him as the summer program progressed. That summer, Stone himself had not been part of the program, as masters often were, and Christopher on his own had gone ahead and made a success of his role in it. He had been popular with the boys, had won over the stubborn cases, and had made real friends. He was showing a new independence; he was no longer George Stone's boy.

In the end, as usual, it was Stuzie who patched things up with a telephone call to George, refusing to allow a small incident such as this to get in the way of a long friendship.

In his last year at Hotchkiss, Christopher and another senior were sent to Groton with Father Kern. They went as representatives of the Hotchkiss Summer GO Program to brief a group of Groton masters and some of the school's sixth formers who had been chosen to inaugurate a similar program in their school. Groton was my school. On their first meeting, George Stone had said to Christopher, "You're the sort of boy we want at Hotchkiss." To us, his parents, George said, "Don't send him to Groton. Groton has a dozen boys like him. We need him at Hotchkiss."

Now, at a critical distance, Christopher was able to look at the school he might have gone to. On that visit, he spoke to perhaps forty people—faculty members, some faculty wives, the prospective proctors. When he described the experience of this trip later, I looked for criticism of my old school. Two friends of mine recently had spoken disparagingly of the place, how small it seemed, how isolated, how removed from real life. By contrast, Hotchkiss in its Go Program had found a way of edging into the mainstream.

But Christopher had many good things to say about Groton. He especially liked the emphasis on making things—on art, on woodwork, and the fashioning of finely turned furniture. He spoke about African-Americans (then "Negroes") in the school. Whereas Hotchkiss had taken boys out of its GO Program—and, deliberately, not always the best boys—Groton had sought out the most distinguished. They were apt to be rich as well as those from a ghetto environment who had demonstrated brilliance. Those Hotchkiss picked sometimes got into trouble or were militantly antagonistic with the result that between the African-Americans and the whites there was poorer feeling than would be found at Groton. Objectively, Christopher wondered whether in the long run, the Groton idea might not be better.

Returning to Fenwick after the GO Program was a letdown for Christopher. Set free in the incomparable freedom of the summer place, he was suddenly without aim or goal, and this very freedom was dispiriting. At dinner, Caroline and I were talking about the uneasiness Christopher was now experiencing. Caroline put it simply, "I think it's because as children, we only had fun in Fenwick."

There were to be some bumps in Christopher's path, including a particularly unpleasant one after his first year in college, a uniquely Sixties bump. During the summer, during an evening with his friends, one of them, a rebellious fellow whose untidy later life confirmed his early instability, surreptitiously spiked their drinks with LSD. Christopher, along with a friend, went on a frighteningly bad trip, hardly knowing what had happened—a trip whose effects, in Christopher's case, lasted for months, inducing a dazed lethargy, forcing him to drop out of college for a year.

I had no comprehension of what it meant to go through such an experience and was stymied in my efforts to relate to it. I recall hearing the writer Rollo May recount the story of his own controlled experiment with LSD. A friend of our across-the-hall neighbors Robert and Nila Magidoff at 165 East Sixtieth Street, Rollo May one evening after a dinner at the Magidoffs described lying on a chaise in a house by the sea in California hearing the waves sound on the Pacific shore while under the influence of the drug. Listening to those waves, he said, returned him to the moment of his birth, the rhythmic movement of the waves recalling the birth pangs of his mother.

I had only a theoretical understanding of Christopher's dilemma, and I recoil now at the thought of how little help as a father I was to a son in trouble.

The uneasy Sixties brought dislocations into the tranquil life of Fenwick. Or was it just that my children—the two older ones—were growing up and growing away? They were not unaffected by what was going on— the Civil Rights movement, drugs, youth rebellion, communal living, moral expediency, the Vietnam War. None of us were.

When one Fenwick son went around the cottages with a young African-American girl soliciting funds for SNCC (the Southern Negro Coordinating Committee), the great national social movement of that period entered cloistered Fenwick. Fenwick was unused to any sort of door-to-door solicitations. Once a summer, a courtly Lebanese gentleman would come into Fenwick with linen and lace goods to show out of the back of his car. He was from the era of our mothers, and his sales dwindled in modern times. Occasionally, a student, usually African-American, would make the rounds on foot offering magazine subscriptions. Watching him proceeding down the shorefront from house to house, one would remain out of sight, guiltily, and ignore his knock on the screen door until he gave up and moved on. From most solicitations Fenwick was removed.

The SNCC girl, however, came sponsored by a Fenwick friend. They were an odd couple, he, keen, intense, athletic, and she, frail-looking and quiet as she sat sinking into our living room sofa. Softly but firmly, with our friend supporting her, she made her irrefutable appeal.

It made me remember the uneasiness I felt when a friend brought the young and then unknown Leontyne Price into our living room in New York one evening. The friend was a member of a Southern family that had known the great singer as a young girl. She was eager to further her career and had helped her with training. And in New York, she wanted friends to know of Miss Price's extraordinary talent. What concerned me was being in the position of patronage to a young black girl whose talent was her only passport to the white world. Miss Price came quite shyly to perform for us. She apologized for being limited by a cold, sat down at our recently bought second-hand upright piano, and sang just for us. That glorious voice nearly lifted the ceiling off our apartment.

In the early years of the 1960s, we sent Caroline off to Denmark (a year abroad which extended to two) to continue her education at the Convent of the Assumption, just outside of Copenhagen. It was here that her mother was sheltered during the war and the Nazi occupation. Some of the sisters she had then known, including the revered Notre Mére, the head of the convent, were still there. So, tearful but confident, we were able to see Caroline leave home with a good heart.

The Denmark experience was a success. She was in the country of her mother's birth. Her mother's Danish cousins accepted her immediately as part of their families. On weekends and holidays, she traveled to Gyldensteen, the great house of the Bernstorff family on the island of Fyn just north of Odense, the town where Hans Christian Andersen was born. The house and its lands lay along the waters of the Kattegat, off the North Sea. Long fields of rye and oats, onions, and potatoes ran down almost to the water's edge. Bente Bernstorff, Stuzie's first cousin, and her husband, Carl

Johann, accepted her as a daughter. The Bernstorff family enfolded Caroline in its warm embrace.

Bente was a tall, quite beautiful, much-admired woman with merry eyes and easy laughter. Her mother, Suzanne Lassen, was the adored aunt of Stuzie's childhood. She wrote and illustrated children's books that had attained a kind of classic status in Denmark. She was as close to Stuzie in her girlhood as Bente was now to Caroline. And Carl Johann, who was some years older than his wife, was a robust, ruddy, large-hearted farmer. Quick-witted and shrewd, he was a model Danish landowner and was as loving to Caroline as a parent.

While Caroline was in Denmark, Suzanne, who was six years younger, remained at home in our apartment on Sixtieth Street and wrote newsy letters to her sister in which the main character might be the elevator man or the superintendent. In one letter, she wrote: "It seems that Christopher likes the seventh-grade girls better than the eighth. He has been to many parties. It is just me and the cats that stay at home."

Staying at home, Suzanne traveled in her mind, and out of her busy head tumbled romances and stories with impossibly glamorous characters of noble pedigrees living on great estates. Very often, her characters were caught up in family quarrels. The children were ungrateful, rebellious. The parents were tyrannical and unloving. At an early age, her typewriter rattled with tales of family conflict. Her stories were neatly typed with chapter headings and page numbers diligently inserted, pages and pages of enthralling narrative continuing on and on with lively incident.

In a family outing one year, traveling in a station wagon out west, Suzanne, then about ten, sat in the back facing the rear window, absorbed in her writing. As we drove through Colorado, Utah, and Nevada, through the Mesa Verde National Park and Zion National Park, past stretches of painted desert, to Las Vegas, she never lifted her head from the typewriter.

I was woefully obtuse, perhaps neglectfully preoccupied, as a father. Her early literary efforts were predictive of an irrepressible narrative imagination I did not then appreciate. Where did those romances come from?

Partly from her mother's storytelling, I think. She had heard the tales of her mother's foreign childhood, the stories of her large family and its eccentric members, and she went ahead creating her own exuberant world on paper.

But I was the cause of some discontent between us. There were scenes, scenes arising from her feeling of being unloved by her father. During an evening in Fenwick in the summer in which she was fourteen, she was sprawled over the desk in the corner of the living room, a pile of papers spread out around her. On some, she had sketched her cartoon-like figures. On others, she had made up games or written the beginnings of stories. It was late. Stuzie and I, tired from too much golf, too much tennis, too much sun and sand and water, were climbing the stairs to go up to bed. We called to her. She made no move to come. So I spoke crossly, all the more so because I knew she would not obey but merely sigh and drop her head over the disordered desk. So I spoke up again, more sharply, and ordered her to clean up her mess.

I was in the middle of one of my obsessions with order, a sign more of dissatisfaction with myself than the state of the house. Everything irritated me: bicycles abandoned on the lawn instead of put away in the garage, sneakers taken off and left in the living room, a chair pulled out of place, magazines scattered about, candy wrappings in the ashtray, cigarette butts in the fireplace—and now the mess of papers on the desk in front of Suzanne. I called to Suzanne again.

"In a minute," she mumbled. And I marched up the stairs without another word.

But in the morning, the desk was clear, and later in the day, Suzanne had an idea. She tried it out first on her mother. And now her mother cautioned her, "Not now. This isn't a good time to tell Daddy. Wait and pick a better time later."

Later, after a few false starts, the time came.

"You know the back room?" she began. "The room off the kitchen? Well, I thought maybe I could make a place for myself there. Rearrange the room and make a place to keep my things and do my writing. A writer needs a place all to herself, away from other people. I don't like to write in the living room with people looking over my shoulder."

I agreed to this, with reservations, and the choking knot in our relationship began to loosen. However, she couldn't really have the whole room to herself. We compromised on a division, and an understanding was reached, for the time being.

All this, while her mother patiently worked to smooth over the prickly father-daughter relationship, calming one side and then the other, trying to break the cycle of cause and effect.

So another day began. Under a July sun, it would be a long, lazy, hot day on the Sound. The water lay flat. Sails flapped listlessly on boom and mast. Off towards the lighthouse breakwater, clusters of neighborly power boats lay idle at anchor. The day was going nowhere. Suzanne was unenthusiastic about swimming. She was slow to learn the breathing techniques essential if one was to swim with confidence. As for golf, a chunky little girl from up the beach was struggling down the walk with a too-large golf bag. She had come to pick Suzanne up for a game.

"She cheats," Suzanne said disgustedly. "She doesn't putt properly. She rolls the ball in."

Suzanne illustrated the technique, drawing the putter across the carpet and guiding the ball into the imaginary hole. Suzanne was not looking forward to the weekly match they were scheduled to play. Swimming and golf were not the sports for Suzanne, but tennis that summer, to my surprise, was. During the week, while I was in New York, she spent hours at the backboard. When we next came face to face on the court, her returns were strong, and in our rallies, we were able to develop rhythm and consistency. She was better than her contemporaries, tried hard, and took the game seriously but still had to overcome a temperament that yielded to discouragement.

Towards the end of Caroline's first year in Denmark, we began to get pleading letters to please send her a little money so that she could join a group of American and foreign students on a trip to Russia. There was little question but that we would approve a move so clearly angled towards self-betterment. We sent the money, and she went off on this new adventure. The party included a number of American boys. With one of them, a boy named Robert, she fell briefly in love. When she came home, she showed photographs of this trip. Our friend, Walter Lord, who knew our family intimately, was present for one of these showings. Caroline provided the setting of each photograph, many of them showing views of Robert. "And there," she would say, "is Robert behind." The necessity for this identification occurred so many times that forever after, when we were reminiscing with Walter, this early love of Caroline's became known simply as "Robert Behind."

Walter was a playful friend to every member of my family. One day, he walked Suzanne, aged eight, up Third Avenue to Rappaport's Toy Store, feeding her a cookie at each intersection to keep her on track and moving along. At the end of the journey, she was rewarded with a toy from the store.

When Caroline was at the Rudolf Steiner School and her class yearbook was in preparation, we inveigled Walter to contribute an ad to the book. Walter's early career, before he wrote *A Night to Remember* and the long list of history books that followed, was in advertising at J. Walter Thompson. The ad copy he wrote for the Rudolf Steiner yearbook featured a completely bogus local restaurant. The headline read, "Rudy's, the Best in Diners."

When Caroline visited our Danish family on the island of Fyn, many times we too made this visit, and the visits usually coincided with some great occasion. Arriving, one crossed a moat into the pebbled courtyard of Gyldensteen. If a car sounded its horn as it crossed the bridge and entered the courtyard, Bente and her husband would be standing on the high arched stairway at the entrance of the house ready to greet their guests. When Caroline was sixteen and attending school in Copenhagen, Bente and Carl Johann asked her to be godmother to their fourth child, Axel. She was overjoyed. We went to Denmark for the celebration. There would be a big party at Gyldensteen, a whole weekend of festivities climaxing in the church christening on Sunday in the small stone church on the property. By Danish custom, there were a number of other godparents: Carl Johann's sister; a friend from Scotland in a kilt; a pretty cousin of Bente's from Sweden; and another cousin, Axel Busche, a German soldier who had lost a leg on the Russian front in World War II and who had been in the Von Stauffenberg bomb plot against Hitler.

Busche, tall and robust with a commanding, no-nonsense manner and international contacts and friendships, had many war stories. One time, in 1940, on the eastern front, there was a dinner gathering of high-ranking German officers. Abruptly, shattering the comradeship of the evening, one officer took out his revolver and fired into a portrait of Hitler on the wall. Immediately, the senior officer present stood up. "The only way we can survive this is for everyone in the room to fire into the portrait." Thereupon, every officer in the room took out his revolver and fired.

There was a great dinner on Saturday night of that weekend with some thirty people seated at the dinner table at Gyldensteen. Carl Johann, a speechmaker to honor the Danish custom of speechmaking, did not disappoint anyone on the occasion of the christening of his third boy and fourth child. There were many high moments in that weekend. On Saturday afternoon, a group of us, including Axel Busche, went down to Gyldensteen's stony beach for a swim. Making his way across the pebbly beach, Axel unstrapped his prosthetic leg, laid it on the sand, and went one-legged into the sea.

On this visit, Carl Johann told me the story of his land. Many thousands of his acres lay along the sea—sandy soil deemed unfit for cultivation. Carl Johann was not convinced. He made a study of seaside land management. He took a trip to Holland to inspect the hydrocultivation of crops there. He persuaded himself that he could utilize his seaside lands to plant crops of grain. The technique was to deep plow the land to intermix the sand with the earth. This was a very expensive operation. He decided to devote a large part of his fortune to the job and take the gamble. He deep plowed along the sea, planted a crop, and waited. The future of Gyldensteen rested on the outcome. The next year, a crop came up. He was vindicated. He went to a jewelry store in Copenhagen and decked his wife with diamonds. "And now," he said proudly. "Now, I can pass Gyldensteen down to my son and my son's son." He was a happy man.

Caroline, in the land of her mother, was a part of this Danish world. And when she grew up, married an Englishman, Jasper Larken, and moved away to London, she visited Denmark often, returning to Carl Johann and Bente at Gyldensteen.

We were present for Carl Johann's last "shoot" at Gyldensteen in December of 1991. For complicated reasons of tax and inheritance, he had decided to turn over the property to his eldest son, Frants, and move to England. As purely an observer, having never handled a shotgun, I was nevertheless included in the hearty shoot lunch in the basement of the manor house. A party of some twenty men sat down on benches at wooden tables for a meal of herring, beef stew, and mashed potatoes, helped down with rounds of schnapps and beer and interrupted by lengthy, laudatory, and emotional speeches in Danish to which I listened intently but could not understand. After this splendid lunch, the party, ruddy with spirits, set out for the shoot, each gun positioned along a line in the forest. Thirty beaters, all farm workers and local men, were sent ahead to raise the birds. For the afternoon drives, I took up a position beside Peter, one of Carl Johann's three sons, and watched as his gun brought down several birds. On this special occasion, Carl Johann paid particular tribute to his gamekeeper of many years, who had arranged so many pleasurable shoots and parties at Gyldensteen. It was an emotional parting. The shoot was a success, mystifying to me, highly satisfying to the participants, but sad for Carl Johann.

With Caroline and her husband, Jasper, we spent New Year's Eve alone with Carl Johann and Bente, their last New Year's at Gyldensteen. In less than a week, they would be away in England. Solemnly, we dressed in evening clothes.

All through the evening, I was uneasily conscious of the break that was to come for the Bernstorffs after so many years on this stretch of Danish soil. We were in a sense family, Stuzie and I, Caroline and Jasper, but not close family, at an occasion that seemed too personal for outsiders, as if we had arrived at the door unexpectedly on a day of mourning. Carl Johann and Bente behaved as cheerfully as if it were just another New Year's Eve.

When Caroline returned from Denmark, she entered the Academy of Dramatic Arts in New York in a class that included Danny DeVito and Michael Douglas, and won the much-prized Jellinger Award in her last year.

In the summer of Caroline's twenty-first year, ahe was working in New York as the store manager of an all-paper dress shop—dresses fashioned 100 percent out of paper—which had been started by a friend, Bill Guggenheim. The enterprise attracted considerable public attention. With the heavy title of vice president, Caroline had been interviewed on radio (that actress training did not go for naught), her picture had been in the paper, and she had taped a television show. In a paper dress, she had addressed a large luncheon of fashion executives, writers, and paper manufacturers. No publicity stunt was too much for the paper business. She once walked down Sixtieth Street, a dog on a lead, dressed entirely in stitched-together dollar bills, top and bottom.

Stuzie had told my father, "I think your granddaughter takes after you. She has a real business head. We are amazed at her. She has a very good sense of where the money is."

This job was a foreshadowing of the stationery business Caroline would start in London some years after she married Jasper. In Fenwick one summer, when computers began to appear, she became interested in what they could do and thought of bringing one home to England where they were still rather rare and where she might be ahead of the game. She began her business by creating a database on her newly purchased computer for the extensive mailing list of a rug cleaner who had just done her carpets. Shortly after that start, she moved into a stationery business that kept enlarging year by year. She showed a command of the business and a flare for handling people, not only those who worked for her but the impatient and sometimes disgruntled customers when an order was late or a typographical mistake had occurred.

One evening in the summer of 1966, without the two older children, Stuzie, Suzanne, and I were sitting in the kitchen in Fenwick. Suzanne was fifteen that summer and going away to school in the fall. Stuzie and I were still eating at the kitchen table, but Suzanne stood apart at the sink. She sprang a question on us: "Why don't I have any confidence? When I have children, how am I going to give them confidence in themselves?"

Temperamentally, Suzanne and I were too alike for me to offer a reasoned response, annoyed as I was at the question. Stuzie gave it a try.

"In the end, you have to find that yourself. No one can really give it to you. You have to find it on your own."

Suzanne persisted in her questions. "Why haven't you given me confidence? Why don't you have confidence yourselves?"

I felt the sharp point of this accusation. It backed me up several days to the aftermath of a birthday party we had given for Caroline in New York. The last of some sixty guests had left around ten thirty. We closed the apartment door on the mess. Stuzie, Suzanne, a friend, and I went up the block to the corner restaurant for a late dinner. (Caroline had gone on with her friends.)

Around midnight, we returned home to find Caroline already back. She had taken off her paper dress. In her slip, she was cleaning up after her party. The dining room table was back in place, the ashtrays emptied, and glasses carried to the sink. In the morning, we were leaving for Fenwick, and I wanted everything straightened up and shipshape. Suzanne was keeping apart from the work, diverting Stuzie and Caroline with comments about the guests and talk about the party. I took out the vacuum cleaner, which raised a clamor of protests. I was making too much noise and disturbing the neighbors below. I resorted to the broom and dustpan. Why did I have to do this when they were just standing around?

"Come on and help me clean up," I said sharply.

Suzanne stood there laughing. "I don't see what there is to clean up, Daddy."

With that, I went into the bedroom and slammed the door. I flung open the windows and looked down on the street four floors below. In my bad period, I was feeling sorry for myself. This was two months after my newspaper, the *New York Herald Tribune*, had folded. Rather than search for a new job immediately and regain my footing, I pursued the idea for a theater magazine. It never did materialize. Now I couldn't get even my youngest child to obey me. Stuzie came into the bedroom, and I cried. She could not help me. When she left, I picked up a glass ashtray and hurled it across the room at the wall. It shattered. From just outside the bedroom door, Caroline came in and dropped to the floor to help me pick up the pieces. I wondered where the ashtray had hit. For the moment, I could not see any scars on the wall. Stuzie had gone to Suzanne, who was afraid and in tears. I knew I would have to face everyone and try to repair the human damage I had done. As I went out of the bedroom, I saw the ugly black marks near the base of the door where the ashtray hit. I went to Suzanne.

"Why don't you have confidence in yourself, Daddy? You must have confidence in yourself."

"But I do," I protested, unconvincingly. "I really do. I have a high opinion of myself."

"No, you don't," she said.

So the same accusations returned, several days later in Fenwick, all over again. At the kitchen sink, half turning to face me, she made a deliberately provocative remark.

"You never play tennis with me anymore."

This was unjust, and I felt like attacking her. Stuzie came to my defense. She was slow to anger, patient, and difficult to provoke, always taking time to talk problems through. At an abrupt order from me, Suzanne came to the table. Suzanne continued to accuse me of neglect, now including her mother unjustly, so unjustly that in a rage, I tried to hit her. Missing, I slammed my open palm ridiculously onto the table top. In fear, Suzanne drew back. Tearfully, she retreated to the dark lower steps of the back staircase. In time, Stuzie went to her.

"Just body love," she said. "Sometimes that's what's needed." And she held Suzanne.

I could not go to her myself just then. But after a while, we led her to the long sofa in the back room, and there, in the semi-darkness, Stuzie comforted her again.

"You think you are very bad, don't you?" Stuzie said softly to her daughter.

"Yes, yes," Suzanne said quickly.

"You are afraid because you think you are bad. How proud we were of you when you were able to admit that you had a bad temper. And you began to see that you had to control it."

There were plenty of reasons later for the parents to have pride in the mind that created those early, easily flowing stories of hers. She pursued a career that led colorfully through a variety of jobs before finally settling into a serious profession. In her days of inquiring uncertainty, as we thought, she wrote jacket copy for Bantam Books, worked for *Publishers Weekly*, wrote for *MS* magazine, and (the one I really love) repaired saxophones for such masters as John Coltrane in Sol Fromkin's shop off Times Square.

Then she decided to study for a doctorate in clinical psychology at the City University of New York, and life changed. She began her professional career with an internship in the psychiatric division of Bellevue Hospital in New York.

When we get together nowadays, the tempo of life picks up. Her humor is playful. (My wife takes credit for insisting that all her children have a sense of humor.) Her interests are strong in art and music. But in a flash, her face can assume an intensity and concentration that are new in Suzanne to me. Talking her game, she turns authoritatively professional.

Chapter 14

On the Water

In the 1960s, my life on the water in Fenwick was limited for lack of a boat. The *Shadow*, the well-loved sailboat of my boyhood, was sold to an upriver buyer. It was painful to see it go, and I avoided looking for it in the river with a new owner at the helm. With three children, I had responsibilities that precluded pursuit of a life under sail. I preserved in memoriam an exact replica model of the boat made to order by a local model builder which my parents had given to me on my sixteenth birthday. It remained as an emblem of long, serene summer days out from land.

I still longed for some access to the Sound and the river and adventures at sea. I was prejudiced in favor of sail over power—"Stink pots" my father called motorboats. But when two boating friends, Sam Jones and Bill Lyon, offered to sell me their nineteen-foot motor launch for a very fair price, I was ready.

The *Buzz*, as she was aptly named, was built for river use as a shad-fishing boat. She had a four-cylinder inboard engine that worked faultlessly at the touch of the starting button; a roomy cockpit with side seats and high coaming; a regular stern tiller; a side tiller as well, located midship on the starboard side, which was handy for maneuvering dockside; and a glassed-in spray screen housing forward. She was workmanlike if not pretty. She made six knots in a calm sea and was remarkably maneuverable, idling at a very low speed. The *Buzz* could cross the Sound in ninety minutes.

I was entirely at home in her from the minute I stepped aboard. I kept her at a mooring in South Cove. From there, all waters were open to me—the river, Hamburg Cove, Selden's Creek, the Sound across to Plum Gut, Greenport, Truman's Beach, and Shelter Island Sound—points from which Fenwick disappeared as a dot on the horizon.

The *Buzz* met the ultimate test by making its way, laboriously, against the racing currents in Plum Gut. In that narrow opening between Orient Point at the tip of the North Fork of Long Island and Plum Island, all the waters of Long Island Sound emptied into the open ocean. If need be, the *Buzz* could withstand heavy seas.

Child of an island kingdom and a seagoing nation though she was, Stuzie was a reluctant sea companion. Gamely, she signed on, along with our daughter Caroline, for one of our longer trips. It took us across the Sound and around Orient Point to Greenport to meet a colleague of mine on the *New York Herald Tribune* who was summering with his family at Southold. Being city folk unaccustomed to the sea, they reluctantly climbed aboard, and we set out, now seven aboard, to visit another colleague on the southwestern shore of Shelter Island. Our friends remained stiffly in their seats, clinging tightly to the side coaming, apprehensive of any strengthening of the breeze. We located the seaside house of our friend on Shelter Island and were waved into his dock where we stepped ashore. The relief on the faces of our distrustful friends as they set foot on solid land was unmistakable.

It was late afternoon when we boarded the *Buzz* again for the return trip. We dropped off our now-relieved friends at Greenport then rounded Orient again to enter the Sound and make our way home. Once past the Gut, moving into the Sound, darkness descended, and we were without traveling lights. Now it was my wife and daughter's turn to be distrustful of the helmsman. The *Buzz* slipped through the dark water under a dark sky. Stuzie and Caroline crouched down in the cockpit, huddling together against the evening chill, and soon fortified themselves with a bottle of bourbon.

The beams of the Outer Lighthouse at the mouth of the Connecticut River, distinctive among all the lights now showing on the home shore, led us in. We made port safely, without incident, much to the surprise of my skeptical passengers.

Many times had I crossed the Sound in the *Shadow*, and for some years in the 1960s, I made that crossing in the *Buzz,* often to cast for bluefish among the rocks against the western shore of Plum Island. Once, to the amazement of Fenwick children, I made the nine-mile crossing in a rowboat. This was not some stunt on my part. It was in the service of a friend who set out one August morning in 1960 to swim across Long Island Sound.

John Chapple, a recent Yale graduate and swimming team member, had for several summers been the swimming instructor for the Fenwick Play Class. He was a powerfully built young man, broad-shouldered and deep-chested. Bright and determined, he seemed to carry a slight undercurrent of discontent that made one want to know him better. He seemed to be testing himself, as if *he* wanted to know himself better.

I was on vacation one Sunday evening at the beginning of August when he came around to the house with Jack Wilson, one of the Play Class parents, to discuss his plan for a cross-sound swim. Off hours, he had been practicing long swims most of the summer, out to the lighthouse or up the shore to Guard House Point, both swims of about a mile in length.

Knowing that I had some knowledge of tidal currents from my sailing days, he enlisted my help in planning the attempt. We met around the dining room table spreading out tidal charts and current tables. We would start from the far side of the Sound, crossing over in Jack Wilson's launch, the *Rujack*. A rowboat would go alongside John to guide him directionally and keep him on course as he swam. I volunteered for that job.

After consulting the charts and tables, I calculated that the optimum time to start the swim would be no later than nine o'clock the following morning. The current on the Long Island shore would still be incoming, moving westward; during the course of the swim, the unfavorable and much swifter outgoing current would be reduced to a minimum. We would be encountering both tides but splitting the difference.

On Monday morning, a heavy fog hung over Fenwick. Gathering at the pier, we were of two minds about making the trip. The launch was ready, stocked with stores, including sandwiches and hot soup. I had my current charts showing the strength and direction of flow at the various hours of the tide. We had my brother's pram, a small rowboat, in tow for me to row. And the fog hung heavily, giving us pause.

This Monday, however, was John's only remaining day off in the summer. Around ten o'clock, we decided to push off and see what conditions were like on the far shore. As we were powering over, we felt chilly and damp. Aboard the *Rujack,* besides Jack, her captain, John, and me, were Jack's children, Hall and Jade, and my son Christopher.

I had fixed on Rocky Point, almost directly across from Fenwick, as the best jumping-off place. Instinctively, I knew we should be further west to account for the currents. But the land to the west fell away into a broad bay, lengthening the cross-sound swim by perhaps half a mile.

When we reached the far shore, we were disappointed to see that fog hung there, too. On the rocks at the point, as I rowed John ashore in the pram, a few fishermen were casting out lines. They regarded us in silence, and we did not explain our intrusion.

John climbed out of the pram and walked along a sandy beach to the outcropping of rocks. Above the beach, on a bluff, stood an abandoned coast guard lookout point still depicted on the charts. The fishermen swung their poles across the water. Clambering from rock to rock, John reached the outermost boulder. He had on blue bathing shorts as brief as a jockstrap. He had covered his chest and limbs with lard. I got back in my pram. The *Rujack* stood off, waiting. The fishermen barely stirred. Off the final rock, John plunged in. It was 11:15 AM.

With smooth, sure strokes, John pulled away from land. In the pram, I moved in alongside, lining up my bow with his left shoulder. For the rest of the trip, I was obliged to hold this position. My job was to steer him and keep him on course. The *Rujack* followed to keep me headed right and to scout the water in front of us and locate chart marks.

According to plan, John swam without stopping for about an hour and three-quarters then stopped to look around, and we had a chance to assess his position. It was obvious to me that we were now in the outgoing tide, which was stronger than we had anticipated. We were barely two miles offshore. To compensate for wind and tide, I directed John in a northwesterly direction, several points on the compass above the straight-line course to our destination, the beach at Fenwick. Now we knew; it would be uphill all the way.

John would swim four strokes together then cock his head to the left to take a breath on the fourth stroke. His eye would come out of the water and look for me. John had forgotten his goggles, and that eye, presented and re-presented, grew progressively redder. No words passed between us, only that momentary locking of eyes again and again.

In the early afternoon, he stopped several times to eat a sandwich, drink soup, and re-lard his body. The food was passed from the *Rujack* to me. John would tread water, holding his arm high above the waves, and I would hand the sandwich to him. Once, I handed down a cup of soup without testing it first and it scalded his throat.

The sun had passed its zenith now, and it was growing colder. We would move soon into September. The southwest breeze was freshening, but the sea wasn't rough. The fog had cleared off. By mid-afternoon, after four hours on the water, we were about halfway across.

The strong outgoing tide was setting us down to the east, past the mouth of the Connecticut River. The two lighthouses were already coming into line. The *Rujack* came alongside. Would we have to give up our hope of landing in Fenwick?

Very soon, we would be slipping east of the mouth of the river, in danger of being caught in its powerful outward rush of water in the ebbing tide. We had to give up the thought of making Fenwick.

Later, John confessed to feeling discouragement at this point. For the first time, in all of us, doubts crept in as to whether we would make it.

As the afternoon lengthened, it grew colder. Sometimes, when he came up for a breath, I tried to speak a word of encouragement. We had to give up our secondary goal of landing in Lyme and fix our hopes on the next promontory to the east, Hachett's Point, where there was a small summer community much like ours.

The sun was setting. We were still several miles offshore. But we had been sighted. Dozens of children and friends from Fenwick were waiting on the beach at Hatchett's.

The last hour of the swim was the hardest. Finally, the shore was in reach. John was still fighting his way in, now very near exhaustion. It was almost eight o'clock at night. He had been in the water nine hours. In the end, he gained by inches only. Rows of silent, awed children lined the beach, and behind them stood the grownups.

We had transferred some blankets from the *Rujack* to wrap around John as soon as he reached the shore. We had no idea what condition he'd be in at the end. My pram touched the sand, and I looked back to see him come in. He took the last strokes strongly and found bottom. He rose to his feet. His black chest hair was matted with lard. His eyes were great reddened holes. The children looked on fearful and silent. Feebly, I called out to them to raise a cheer for John. But everyone was struck dumb. On legs that weighed heavily, he walked ashore. I threw the blankets around his shoulders. A friend offered him a bottle of whisky. Reluctantly, for his disciplined training had ruled out liquor, he took a swallow. The bottle was handed to me, and I tipped it back.

The children, now noisy and celebrating, followed him up the beach. He was taken to a house where a hot bath was drawn. The children had looked at me with some wonder too, because I had rowed across the Sound. I, too, was a hero of that day. Together, John and I had traveled not the straight-line nine-mile width of the Sound but perhaps, in our diagonal crossing, some twenty miles in all.

After the bath, John was in fine spirits. A series of parties were held in Fenwick from house to house all evening in celebration of his achievement. John showed no ill effects from his long swim. As for me, as a penalty for my bravado in rowing across the Sound, I suffered a tennis elbow in my left arm for a year for pulling on that oar, and the arm remains the first part of me to succumb when I suffer a periodic attack of my rheumatoid arthritis, but it was a small penalty for witnessing the greatest physical feat I had seen in my lifetime, and for sharing in it, too.

Late in my seventies, I was seized with a desire to be on the water again. The *Buzz* had long since been decommissioned, and I was land bound. I sent for the catalogue of the New York Kayak Company located on Pier 40 just a few blocks from our loft in SoHo.

The kayak is about the smallest vessel you can go to sea in. It's just a hull with a paddle and a cockpit with a spray skirt fitting snugly to the coaming to protect against choppy seas. You are alone in your boat watching each approaching wave with a cautious eye and sitting no more than inches above the water, knees braced against the gunwales to steady the craft, and feeling every motion of the sea throughout your body.

With heady thoughts of trips to come, I went over to Pier 40 and bought the 14'9" Feathercraft Kahuna whose black hull and bright yellow decking I had admired in the catalogue. A collapsible kayak, disassembled, it could be stored in a bulky blue bag and carried from place to place. The instruction book said its anodized aluminum frame could be fitted into the polyurethane skin around the four polycarbonate cross ribs and the whole kayak assembled in twenty minutes. I laid out the parts on our loft floor. The trial assembly took me a week. Even then, I had to hire a man to help me perform the most difficult operation—fitting the aluminum gunwale rods into the notches at the top of the cross ribs under extreme tension. In time, assembly would be reduced to only a few hours.

That first kayaking summer in Fenwick, with a companion, I warily crossed the Connecticut River, braving its running currents and channel traffic to reach the Lyme shore and move around and through the great ornithologist Roger Tory Peterson's Great Island where the osprey nest. One could glide through the narrow cuts in the island so silently that the birds barely noticed. One felt an affinity in nature for all above the water and all below it. The kayak, so simple in structure, opened a world hidden to faster traveling boats. On the avenues of New York for thirty-five years, the bicycle had been my principal form of transportation. There had been some bumps and bruises over the years, but nothing to dampen the exhilaration of pedaling my own way. Now I had this same joy on the water. The kayak would move only when you lifted the paddle. And the swiftness and the distances one could travel without exhaustion even at my age were remarkable.

Kimberly J. Heyl

Afloat off Great Island

The portability of the Feathercraft tempted me to plan a special trip away from my own waters. The next summer, we were going to Denmark to visit Skagen at the northernmost tip of Jutland and see Danish relatives. Skagen is land's end in Denmark, a small fishing town distinguished for having once been the summer site of a school of nineteenth-century painters headed by Krøyer, one of Denmark's finest artists. Its outermost point ends in a sandbar shaped like a panhandle that divides two bodies of water, the Skagerrat and the Kattegat, just off the North Sea. Where they come together, the waters rise up in foam and sea caps. The treacherous cross currents off this point have caused many ships to founder. Their retrieved nameplates ring the walls of a solemn room in a Skagen museum devoted to the rescue efforts of heroic local fishermen.

I thought if I could trundle my kayak on its carry-cart through the airports of Newark and Copenhagen, I could transport it by rail or car to

Skagen off the North Sea. There, I could float it in the more protected waters on the lee side of the point and come home and boast that I had "kayaked in the Kattegat." As I was in my ninth decade, I thought this might at the very least impress a few friends. My wife felt that I should have acquired the kayak several decades earlier in my life. As to her opinion of my present plans, well, she deemed them a case of misplaced bravado.

With some difficulty and with the helpful intervention of Stuzie's Danish niece Suzanne, who enlisted the services of a Copenhagen trucking company, I was able to get the kayak to Skagen.

Gale winds greeted us on arrival. We were at once in touch with another cousin, Anne-Sophie Nyegaard, whose husband, Henrik, had been coming to Skagen since he was twelve. In all his years, he said, he had never seen it blow so hard. In the landscape of that flattened sandspit, his cottage was hunkered down between protecting dunes.

"We have bad news for you," he greeted me as I arrived at his door for an update on the weather. "Anne-Sophie has been in touch with the local kayak club. They said it was impossible to think of going out, and they expect these winds to continue all week."

That essentially ended my kayaking plans for Skagen. But there were still the museums to visit in compensation. What made me want to go to Skagen in the first place were the painters themselves. The school of Danish painters of the late 1800s lived and dined together in Brøndum's Hotel, whose dining room, with its frieze of portraits ringing the wainscoting of the room, has been recreated in the museum down to the linen-covered dining table. The daughter of the hotel-keepers, Anne Ancher, living among painters, married one, and became one herself; in fact, she was one of Denmark's best of this period. Krøyer depicted a Skagen very different from the one we were experiencing: couples in formal clothes promenading down the beachfront and gazing out on a quiet sea softened by the late summer light. That had been my picture of Skagen.

There was another side. In the museum, Krøyer had large canvases of open lifeboats launched by Skagen fishermen in dangerous surf to rescue the crews of ships wrecked at sea. Now my kayak at least would not run the risk of being in that number.

Back it went to Copenhagen and home to New York to our storage space in the basement of our building on Prince Street without ever having left its bag.

Chapter 15

Home Improvements

Before she died, my mother was determined to have the Fenwick cottage put in good condition so that we would not face any extraordinary expenses when we took over. The cottage had not been re-shingled in years. It showed the wear of seaside weather. It was not easy to find a carpenter who would undertake the sizeable job of re-covering the whole cottage; nor were proper shingles so easy to come by—not cheaply in any case. But my mother persisted. Through the borough office, she found the man who could take on the job. Eventually, the long, laborious work was done. The old shingles were scraped off and new cedar shingles nailed in place throughout the exterior of the cottage. The old place looked as good as new.

In actual fact, the cottage, for all its years, was in good shape. When the architects came in to do the remodeling job we were able to afford when my father's estate was settled, they pronounced its health good. It was a sounder building, they said, than many later constructions of similar cottages. This was reassuring, especially when we planned for greater use of the cottage and a life that would extend, along with our own as a family, down one more generation.

In 1974, however, we gave up Fenwick for another of our visits to Stuzie's home country, and in a month-long stay in Denmark, we made a pointedly symbolic trip to her "ancestral" home.

My father-in-law's failure to inherit Aalholm occasioned a split in the family that lasted for years. This was not due entirely to the division of the property. Little communication had passed between the two brothers in their youth, partly because Siegfried was Johann Otto's senior by twelve years. In World War II, because of differing views on Denmark's role, the break became irreversible, bringing a total silence observed in large part by most members of the respective families. The bad family blood preoccupied and distanced everyone. Some family secrets are more public than others. Since Aalholm was one of the largest estates in Denmark, it hardly escaped notice that the entire property, with its lands and far-flung manor houses, was in the hands of the younger brother when custom and expectation would have entrusted it to the elder.

My wife was determined to break the long years of silence. She resolved that we as a family would make the trip to Aalholm, meet with Johann Otto, and show that on our part, the bad feeling was over. In the younger generation, some contact already existed. My thirty-year-old daughter Caroline, during her year in school in Denmark fifteen years earlier, had became friends with her cousin Vicki Raben, Johann Otto's daughter by his second marriage. Through Vicki, Caroline also met her brother Johnny, Johann Otto's chosen heir. (Freddie Raben, Johann Otto's elder son by his first marriage and a favored cousin of Stuzie, was not to inherit the great property.)

Thanks to Johnny Raben, we had an invitation to lunch at Aalholm on Sunday, August 5. We were staying that summer at Gavnø in Sjaelland, the home of Stuzie's old friend Axel Reedtz-Thott. Axel had died unexpectedly the previous winter. His daughter Elizabeth had kindly seen that our summer plans to visit Gavnø went ahead, and so we were there as a family, staying in one of the houses and enjoying the gardens and park of that large property.

To confirm the arrangements of the visit before starting out from Gavnø, Stuzie had called Aalholm the day before. When the phone was answered, she said, "Is that Johnny?" A voice came on the line, and she inquired again, "Is that Uncle Johann Otto?"

The cryptic answer came back, "I suppose you could say so." There was some humor in the response. There was also a note of reluctance, of something withheld.

The five of us in our family set out from Gavnø on a Sunday morning in August; Stuzie's sister, Charlotte, who was staying with us, elected not to go. Charlotte's important mission on this trip to Denmark was to scatter the ashes of their mother, who had died earlier in the year, and she planned to visit Aalholm later and do it there.

We took the Vordingborg road from Naestved on the island of Sjaelland, crossing on the long bridge to the island of Falster, where we met hitchhikers heading for camping grounds and two parties of cyclists draped in ponchos against the light rain that was falling. On another bridge, we crossed over to Lolland and headed south to the town of Nysted where Aalholm sits, looking across a narrow strait to Germany. A church spire in Nysted rising above the flattened country beckoned us on. We followed a sign leading to the Raben Auto Museum, where Johann Otto's famous collection of classic cars attracted busloads of tourists from Germany. To the left, halfway down the road through an avenue of lime trees, the square towers and sienna-colored walls of Aalholm appeared.

Aalholm sits on its watery spit of land subdued into the landscape, dipped in its colors, brown as the earth, green as the water, the ghost of a house. The postcards and pictures cannot suggest its antiquity, nor can the modern arena-like auto museum demean or alter its great heavy cloak of age. The streams of tourists from Germany cannot by so much as a ripple disturb its ancient tranquility. It is too old to be beautiful, too much a part of nature to be ugly. It is simply there, having endured nearly nine centuries on its watery strand—Aalholm, home of eels. The image of its name is fitting, that of a prehistoric fish, sinewy and strong, at home in darkness.

We turned off the road and headed up the drive. Aalholm, a moated castle, once a Viking fortress, is on the edge of an inlet opening to the sea. Within a second gate as one approached, along a private drive, were a pond and a swimming pool. Beside the pool, a tall figure was absorbed in some chore of inspection. Clearly, it was Baron Johann Otto Raben-Levetzau. He did not look up as we passed. We turned once again in the drive, the inlet on our right, and stopped in the courtyard. Everyone agreed, "Let's get out quickly."

Johann Otto came up to greet us. He was tall and broad-shouldered, with light hair brushed severely back. He had the prominent Raben nose and rather small eyes. He did not smile easily. His manner was formal. He wore a greenish-colored suit. He addressed Stuzie first and then shook hands with each of the children, taking trouble over each name.

We stood there in the U-shaped courtyard looking up at the ivy-covered walls of the castle. On one wall was an odd protruding triangular shaped projection of windows, a late addition oddly out of place. Noticing our questioning looks, Johann Otto described it as an add-on and a pleasant place to sit looking out over the water.

Johann Otto's wife of the last four years, Elizabeth, came out of the house to meet us. She was a Bermudian, who, in one of two previous marriages, had lived in Bedford Village, New York. She was in a bright print dress. We were led into the house for drinks and lunch, passing through a large library room walled with tall bookcases whose top shelves were reachable only by ladder.

We came to a sort of sunroom with a bar looking over the pond and were offered drinks. Johnny Raben appeared with his tall, striking-looking sister, Vicki. Johnny was shorter than his father, wore a moustache, and obviously shared his father's interests, especially in cars. He seemed to have his father's business sense. Johann Otto had little of a personal nature to say to any of us. The occasion, to him, was perfunctory, and his mind seemed preoccupied with business matters such as the expected attendance that afternoon at the auto museum. In fact, it was there he wanted to take us directly after lunch. Instead, we were eager to see the rooms of the castle where Stuzie had played as a girl, where she had walked hand in hand with her loving grandfather, and where she was watched over by the faithful family butler, Oscar, and whose stories of Aalholm in her telling had become part of our family memory. It was almost as if Johann Otto, by prodding us toward the auto museum, which was his own creation, wanted to separate us from the castle, where his own legitimacy was questioned. Our presence might have reawakened old uncertainties.

It was Elizabeth who offered to take us around the castle while her husband went off to attend to other matters. She had drilled herself in the story of the castle and, like any museum guide, delivered her commentary without regard to the nature of her audience. In this, she made a perhaps forgivable misjudgment, for as she threaded her way through the familial interconnections as represented by the portraits and as we passed through the great state rooms, Stuzie, from time to time, interrupted her remarks with corrections, more for our benefit than Elizabeth's.

The house was arranged for tourist visits. On a rose-colored carpet, the great table in the dining room was laid for thirty guests with gleaming linen and shining silver. Across the central fireplace was a needlepoint screen with the family names of the current generations stitched around the border. Anastazia was misspelled with an "s" instead of a "z."

Elizabeth, in her neat print dress, her hair carefully done up, led us from room to room, pointing out objects of interest. Stuzie later felt badly about her interruptions, for Elizabeth was relatively new to the game (following Johann Otto's two previous wives). She had dutifully studied Aalholm history to learn about her own new station in life and deliver her lectures to parties of visitors. Not perhaps fully realizing the depths of the rift that had opened between the families of the two brothers, she yet appeared to have accepted an obligation to be solicitous to us. As it was, as we continued with the tour, all of us were conscious that we may never, any of us, pass this way again.

Now it was Johann Otto's turn. It was obvious that he wanted to divert our attention from the house. Briskly, he suggested that we should visit the auto museum. In his red car, he took us down the old drive in the rain to the museum. Here, the scene changed abruptly. There were buses and cars and crowds of people. Without the attraction of the classic cars, Johann Otto explained, the tourists would never bother to visit the house. The lack of such a diversion, he felt, was the reason many great Danish estate owners failed to generate enough revenue to keep up their properties.

In the enormous shed of the museum, dozens of classic cars were lined up, both American and European. Johann Otto proudly showed them off. The collection was started after the war when he discovered a 1911 Rolls Royce once used by the family in a barn at Beldringer, a manor house belonging to Aalholm where, incidentally, my wife was born. The car had been walled in behind a partition for years. From that relic, the collection grew, with American models added to the European, until it became one of the greatest aggregations of classic cars in Europe.

Johann Otto pointed out his personal favorite, a 1920s pearl-grey Locomobile open sports car with an elongated engine hood, gracefully curved fenders, and large wheels.

Johann Otto was not without the Raben humor. In him, it was not especially generous or outgoing, but rather shrewd and appraising. Ahead of us, two short, plump women were walking down the aisle between the two rows of cars, conversing. One wore a hat that was no more than a circular cardboard band.

"German," Johann Otto declared. "Who but a German would wear a hat like that?"

Stooping over them from his height, he dropped his head into their conversation for an instant to confirm his supposition.

"German, all right," he said, returning.

Outside, on a track that skirted the shore, a small train drawn by an 1870 steam engine left and returned to the exhibition area. Rain from the roof of the museum shed fed the boiler. Johann Otto pointed out to us that no one who had not paid admission to the auto museum could ride the train.

"The average visitor to the auto museum," Johann Otto said, "spends two kroner at the souvenir stand where they have an absolutely worthless collection of souvenirs."

Still, he explained, no one goes away without a postcard of a classic car or of the train to commemorate his visit to the Raben Collection.

We ourselves left without making any purchases. Our day at Aalholm had ended. After saying our good-byes, we got into our car and, happy in our visit, made the journey home to Gavnø. We had seen Aaholm, perhaps never to return.

In the seventies, our life centered more and more on the cottage in Fenwick, particularly when we came into full ownership, my sister having inherited the back lot and my brother the other house up the beach into which my father and mother moved in their last years in Fenwick.

We were obliged to look at the cottage in a new light. Built in the early 1880s by a family from Middletown, Connecticut, and bought by my father in 1920, it seemed to us now less a pleasant vacation diversion from city life and more a fixed home. Almost unconsciously, we were making a shift from regarding our home in New York as the center of family life to the cottage in Fenwick. Fenwick cottages were beginning to be winterized to make them potentially year-round homes. Now we were prepared, financially and psychologically, to do the same. We needed to sit down with architects to plan a new role for the cottage.

We found the ideal man for the job in Ralph Wolfe, a college roommate of my son Christopher, who was now in his second year at the Yale Architecture School. Ralph knew the family. He was sympathetic and sensitive and a friend. In college, he was very much a child of the sixties, and I remember on first meeting, walking with him and Christopher outside the Yale Bowl before a football game, being put off by his shoulder-length black hair.

We began a series of conversations with Ralph and the school classmate he picked to collaborate with him, Mike Lipkin. Together, they would serve not only as architects on the job but also as general contractors and carpenters. The first requirement was to make the cottage livable in all seasons, even with the chill of a seaside winter when the sun was pale and the northwest winds howled across the open back field. With a cottage constructed to be cool, this was not an easy assignment. We would require insulation under the ground floor and in the attic, but also in the side walls through injections of tripolymer foam. Doors would require weather-stripping, and storm windows would be fitted in all the heated rooms. And we would have to decide which areas could be heated and which left in their summer state. Plumbing and heating and the installation of an oil burner would, in monetary terms, be the largest single items of the renovation. But new roofing was required, a third layer over the existing two, reaching the legal limit. Masonry work on the rear chimney of the house was scheduled, and, finally, it would need an exterior repainting.

The chief architectural element of the renovation was the complete redesign of the kitchen into a room for family living. Here, the young architects allowed their imaginations full play, and we along with them. This was their first professional architectural commission. They plunged into the project like professionals. In acknowledgment of that, we did keep out of their way, fully accepting their plans, even when they came to me, apologetically, and said they would have to entirely eliminate a favorite room and workplace of mine. It was also the room Suzanne had picked as a place to do her own writing in private.

The old kitchen would be completely torn out and rebuilt from floor to ceiling. A dropped ceiling was to become the room's most distinguishing feature, and when I first saw it up, I knew for certain we had in these two young students promising architects of imagination and daring. It consisted entirely of unpainted two-inch strips of lath laid an inch apart. This ceiling, in a zebra-stripe pattern, covered the existing exposed plumbing lines in the room. The construction lowered the height of the room but created a compensating airiness and lightness that actually gave a once-dark kitchen greater depth.

A chimney in the kitchen that once served an old coal-burning stove was re-pointed and a Jøetel stove installed. Three logs in the stove could heat the room. The bright flame in the slit of the nearly closed door vent was always a cheering sight. Along one wall, our friends constructed a floor-to-ceiling bookcase. Over the top shelf, imbedded in the construction, was a long neon tube to light the shelves. This installation, the architects confessed, was their one major construction blunder. If the neon tube burned out, the only way to remove and replace it was to drill a hole at the end of the bookcase and draw the long, unbendable tube out a back kitchen window. Sure enough, ten years later, we had to execute this awkward maneuver.

The work commenced in May and continued into the summer. Ralph and Mike and their girlfriends lived in the house. We would receive weekly progress and expense reports in Ralph's neat architect's script, and I would replenish the drawing account I put in their control in a Westbrook bank. Watching the money run out for such a purpose was almost a pleasure. It seemed to be going fast. Yet it was money in the service, we felt, of a large creative idea, in the service of creating a permanent, lasting, and livable home. And when all the accounts were added up, including the payroll for the extra carpenters Ralph and Mike brought in from time to time when the workload increased and the schedule tightened, the total in the dollars of those years—design, labor, and materials—came to slightly less than $35,000.

As the work proceeded, our conception of the house changed. Gradually, it was becoming more our house, and we imagined a larger role for it in our lives. It was always a refuge from the city; its sheltering walls made it livable even in winter now, and we began to recognize it as a more substantial home than our Sixtieth Street apartment. Now the remodeled house would take care of us.

Remodeling a house from the inside is probably more difficult than constructing a new house from scratch. While preserving the integrity of the house as a whole, such work involves the reshaping of space, the removal of walls, and the elimination of some rooms altogether. An example, in our case, was the cozy, closet-size telephone room where we hung coats, stored tennis racquets and golf clubs, and where, momentously in our family, my father in the 1930s, when our telephone exchange number was in two digits, received a business call from Australia. In the narrow space, we children crowded around to be as close as possible to this unheard-of continent-bridging telephone connection which left even the Saybrook operators open-mouthed, as my father struggled in his deafness to catch the message imperfectly transmitted from so far away.

Planning these changes to the cottage and then watching as they were realized step by step gave us unreasonable pleasure. On the outside, but for the new paint job—forest green and maroon trim—the cottage was unchanged. Most of the improvements were invisible from the outside, except for two skylights, one to light the kitchen, the other in parallel in the hall, which was separated from the kitchen by a glass insulating wall. The single most thrilling moment in the construction cycle came one day when the low roof over my old workroom was ripped open and we could see through to the sky. Forever after, sitting beneath those wondrous skylights, I marveled at being able to gauge in the snugness of the kitchen the state of the day from the movement of the clouds across those narrow strips of Plexiglas.

Christopher Little

The new kitchen with its zebra-striped drop ceiling

In those years, for extra income, we rented the house for the month of July. By the time Jack and Cynthia Rehm arrived with their family on the first of the month, it was hoped our team would be largely finished with the work. Of course, they were not. As the Rehm family unloaded their suitcases, a table saw stood in the middle of the kitchen and sawdust was thick on the floor. Greeting Jack, who was chief executive of Meredith, one of the largest magazine publishing houses in the country, I suggested jokingly that perhaps he would like his money back. He smiled and moved in. The Rehms were in fact model renters. Each year, when they returned the house to us on the first of August, however much they may have moved furniture around to suit themselves, every piece was back in its accustomed place, even to the order of odd objects arranged on the mantelpiece. The Rehms endured the intrusion and inconvenience, which lasted the whole month, with no complaint and with surprising good humor, entering themselves into the spirit of the renovation as if it were an improvement to a house of their own.

There is some irony here. The Rehms subsequently bought a small cottage in Fenwick and in time created two architecturally distinctive additions to this cottage that tripled its size. It would not have occurred to me in those busy, hopeful days of building that in seventeen years, we would have sold our cottage. The new owner, in making over the house, obliterated our handsome new kitchen as well as every other improvement we had made. And meanwhile, the family that had been but renters in my house at the time of these alterations made such significant architectural improvements to their house as in retrospect to make our hopeful renovation seem merely makeshift and stopgap.

There was a further irony. That first winter, after everything was completed, we lent the house to a friend, who was then living with a young woman while his wife, from whom he would shortly be divorced, occupied his own cottage in full view of ours across two back lots. Twenty years later, we would consider ourselves fortunate to be renting *his* cottage to maintain our summers in Fenwick.

After the final reckoning of accounts and after we had a chance to experience the remade cottage, Ralph and I had an exchange of letters, I to thank and compliment him on his fine work, he to express to me his own feelings.

One clear message of his letter is the apprehension I suppose every architect feels that the job is unfinished until it meets the test of time. This feeling was, as Ralph suggested, only heightened by his continuing association with us through friendship. He wouldn't be going away; he'd still be accountable.

The redoing of the cottage, as he said, was a shared experience, so closely shared, in fact, that when the work was completed, the pride of ownership competed with the pride of creation. Just whose new kitchen was it, ours or Ralph's? Is it the architect's house or is it the owner's?

We continued almost annually to make small improvements to the house, as the bank balance would allow, and one major one. With a clever female contractor from Lyme, we laid out a new scheme for the west porch—the one my father claimed sotto voce as the best porch in Fenwick. On hot days, it caught whatever southwest breezes were circulating. Because it was an open porch with a half wall around it and screens above, it was unusable in rainy or cold weather. We declared summer at an end when it was time to take down those porch screens and stack them in the house until the following spring.

Around the open west porch, we installed full-length sliding patio doors with double-pane glass. When the job was completed and floor heating and new electricity lines were installed, we had a porch that was serviceable night and day and in every kind of weather. Other than the new kitchen, it became the most lived-in part of the house.

Only two years after the major Fenwick renovation was completed, after thirty-two years in New York on Sixtieth Street, we moved to our loft on Prince Street in SoHo. It had only recently been redone for a woman artist by a famous New York graphic designer, the late Herbert Lubalin, who created a typeface that bears his name. Lubalin kept the integrity of the interior, cleaning the three great ten-inch-square posts that ran down the middle of the sixty-foot room and the twelve-inch bearing beams to a fine burnt umber in color. Some of the walls were given a rough-textured plastering, and others were paneled with oak flooring. Lubalin created a kitchen in the high-tech mode of that time with file cabinets for storage drawers, white Formica-lined cabinets with glass shelves, and a tiled kitchen floor—all in pristine condition. Then, when it was all done, he persuaded the owner to marry him and move to his house a few blocks north in Macdougal Alley, putting the loft on the market and presenting us with a remarkable opportunity. Five minutes after we stepped into the place, we agreed to the listed price.

For us, there was only one problem with the loft as it stood—there was no bookcase anywhere. Not wishing to introduce anything disharmonious to Lubalin's design, I asked him to show us where to place the bookcases. Briskly, he indicated one suitable wall. On a sheet of paper, standing up, he sketched out for a corner of the room a place for my desk with a bunk bed above it and another bookcase on the wall. So, to this splendid loft, with its five large southern windows, which was to be our home for twenty-seven years, we had made some additions of our own. The space that was conceived for someone else had become ours.

Living in a place actually transforms it in one's mind so that even its design begins to assume a familiarity as if it had always been one's own. Greater than the sum of its parts, the Fenwick renovation took on a symbolic significance. Although I was then in my fifties, awakening, really for the first time, to the realization of some limitations on my life, the future seemed limitless. We were born again in the new house.

Chapter 16

Rushing through the Nineteen Nineties

Like many small towns in Connecticut, Old Saybrook, while very much a blue-collar town, is rock-ribbed Republican. God knows Fenwick is too. This does not mean that Old Saybrook and Fenwick are in lockstep politically or socially. The town, one imagines, looks across the causeway at the privileged little community of summer folk with suspicion, possibly envy, maybe distrust. From Fenwick's side, in different ways, the suspicion is reciprocated, although it's probably true to say that Fenwick, for the most part, gives less thought to the town than it should.

The warden of the Borough of Fenwick, as its chief governing officer, has to pay more attention than the rest of us to the town and its officers, especially the first selectman, in deference to town-borough relations. On our behalf, he has to keep an eye on town politics and policies as they affect the borough and try on even terms to conduct a dialogue with his town counterpart. Aside from the warden in our community, one or two civic-minded citizens made very real contributions to the life of the town. This may have been partly due to the aristocratic notion that the enjoyment of the special privileges to be found in the borough carried the consequent responsibility of giving back something to the mother town.

They were not inconsiderable gifts. Marion Grant wrote a town history. Her husband, Ellsworth, produced a film about the Connecticut River (narrated by his sister-in-law Katharine Hepburn), illuminating the problems and possibilities of this great waterway. He helped lead the effort to create a public park at Saybrook Point to mark Saybrook Fort. Oliver Jensen, a founding editor of *American Heritage* magazine, created the Valley Railroad on old riverside tracks with authentic steam locomotives and vintage parlor cars to establish one of the chief tourist attractions of the area. Others played a role in the life of the town library or of the Old Saybrook Historical Society.

Most of the rest of us coasted along at our ease from summer to summer, counting moments spent shopping in town as lost to the pleasures that were to be found in Fenwick, happy once we had crossed the causeway and were securely inside the borough again.

Fenwick's borough form of government insulated us from some aspects of town control, although not all. Governed by a warden and burgesses, it had taxing power, zoning authority, and a park commission, which, to an extent, could specify the use of our nine-hole golf course, although it was a public course open to the town.

But Old Saybrook held the ultimate control—the town real estate tax. For years, that didn't bother Fenwick property holders all that much—not until the end of the 1980s, that is, when Fenwick property was reassessed. The work was to be done by an out-of-state firm hired by the town, and the outlook for Fenwick was ominous. When the figures were finally posted, the results were even more shocking than expected, and waterfront property, whether on the Sound, river, or cove, was hit heavily. That meant us.

The whole community joined together to contest the punishing assessments in court in Middletown, but this attempt went nowhere. Finally, the Hartford lawyers representing the Fenwick landowners en masse were reduced to making a blanket settlement proposal that would have reduced land evaluations by 15 percent. And even that was rejected out of hand by the town. No other offer, it was made clear, would be entertained. One angry landowner initiated an action of his own, also fruitlessly. To make my own case, I appeared before the Board of Tax Review in Town Hall in Old Saybrook on March 13, 1990. My argument was that the situation of my house on the shore was more vulnerable to sea assault than that of my neighbors on either side, both of whom enjoyed higher ground but tax liability no greater than mine. My western neighbor's higher landfill even contributed to the flooding of my property in a southerly storm.

The review board disregarded this argument. Nor was it in the slightest degree moved by the evidence of vulnerability in the pictures I produced of the damage done to our cottage in the hurricane of 1938. Almost before I began, the cause was lost. On our property, the reassessment would cause a three-fold increase in our taxes. The rest of Fenwick's property owners, most of them in a far better position than I to absorb the increase, protested just as loudly and just as futilely. With her large stretch of waterfront property, even Katharine Hepburn joined the chorus of dissent. I could sense then that the big increase might be a breaking point for me, that there was no protection any longer for a way of life that for years I had taken for granted. In all of us in my family, the attachments to the place were strong, as strong as any other influence in our lives. This was true of me. It was true also of Stuzie, who was homeless in America without this home. She was most in despair at the thought of losing her garden.

For the English family, for Caroline and Jasper and for their children, the annual visit for the month of August was an unbroken ritual. Caroline, our firstborn, had moved to England as the young bride of a strong-willed husband. In time, she came into her own, acquiring a self-reliance that served everyone around her. Partly this may have been due to founding and managing her small, successful business dealing day to day with suppliers and customers. Although an ocean apart, we never lost touch. She included us, her parents and her siblings, in every aspect of her life and included ours in hers.

The grandchildren, Melissa and Jonathan, had come to Fenwick since birth. Fenwick was their nursery. As newcomers and foreigners, they had survived the initial coolness of their American contemporaries. They had survived the derision with which, initially, their English accents were met. They had achieved solid places for themselves.

But it was for only a month, one-twelfth of the year. And these grandchildren, growing up, starting careers, would have less and less of a chance to be there.

Rightly or wrongly, I was less concerned about our other two children. Both Christopher and Suzanne had lives that kept them away from Fenwick. Christopher was eventually to give up his apartment in the city, loosen his connections to Fenwick, and commit fully to the country. Christopher and his wife Betsy moved from Colebrook, where they had made a home in the northwest corner of Connecticut, to a new lakefront house in the adjoining town of Norfolk. After training as an EMT, Christopher joined the Norfolk ambulance corps, surviving parochial judgments of him by his colleagues as a city fellow. He came to straddle the divide between town people and weekenders. Aided by a natural refusal to prejudge, he got along with everyone and showed a charmed interest in every little local happening. Suzanne then was absorbed in the arduous academic exercise that led to her doctorate in clinical psychology.

Maybe I was wrong to take comfort in Christopher's settled position in the country. Christopher still had strong feelings for Fenwick, much the same as mine, and old childhood friendships rooted there. Betsy did not. She came from the country and now lived forty miles from Dalton, Massachusetts, where she grew up. She had made a success in the real estate business in Colebrook and Norfolk and a place for herself in both communities.

One evening a few years ago, Christopher came to the loft with a stack of three-by-five colored photographs showing forty acres of land he and Betsy had just bought in Norfolk where one day, they would build a house. Did his possession of land ease my sense of guilt at selling Fenwick out from under him? I still remember the catch of breath I felt when he and I were discussing the decision to sell, and Christopher had said, "That is not the way I would have handled it." I never summoned the courage to ask him how he would have handled it.

Wasn't there a similar disappointment implied when, on the same subject, my son-in-law in London telephoned for the kindest of reasons and said formally, "We want you to know we are 100 percent behind you in this decision."

Did these reactions make me doubt my decision? They made me regret that I lacked the resources to keep the cottage up. It made me regret that financially, I had not lived up to the responsibility of carrying us through to another generation. The money I would realize from the sale would secure my future while depriving us all of Fenwick as we knew it. It was a hard trade-off but inescapable. I would live with the consequences. So would we all. Once again, I would compare myself with my father.

My father had managed. I thought of the way he had set up the Fenwick property—two cottages and a lot that could be built on for three children. It was a handsome inheritance. My father was a realist. On matters of inheritance, he knew that families, however close, could be broken apart. Each of us three children was happy in this inheritance. All we had to do was take care of our share and maintain it.

In mid-August 1993, we circulated a letter to the residents of Fenwick offering them the opportunity to buy before we put the cottage on the open market.

After the decision to sell, it was easy to come up with rationalizations. We could legitimately complain of our vulnerability to the hurricanes that periodically battered our shore. A hurricane-damaged house would be virtually impossible for us to put right as my father was able to do after 1938. We lived in apprehension of a recurrence of such a storm.

Maintenance of the old cottage was never-ending. Every time one put the key in the door at the end of winter, one faced a certain expenditure of three to five thousand dollars in emergency repairs—rain gutters blown off in a winter's storm, a crumbled section of the seawall to fix, a chimney in need of pointing, a new boiler for the furnace. In future assessment years, taxes would go up again.

How could one justify maintaining at such expense a house one used for only a few months of the year? It was either live in New York or live in Fenwick full-time, and we didn't want to give up New York. I looked for reasons to detach myself from Fenwick. Open though Fenwick was, everyone at bottom had a sense of his own turf. All cottages were not equal.

Fenwick was incestuously interrelated. There were cousins, it seemed, in every cottage (although they were not my cousins). But cousins were not necessarily allies. Where there were relatives, one would also find inter-family rivalry. The chapel, to be sure, was run ostensibly along non-denominational lines, but in form and belief, it was essentially Episcopalian. The religious schisms in the community were real. It was all right to talk about equality; all you had to do to belong was to live within the borough. Nevertheless, distinctions were made.

In my impending separation from Fenwick, the unexpressed drawbacks of the place were uppermost in mind. Lastly, Fenwick had changed. An important part of what held us to Fenwick was no longer there. That special coterie that made the place so pleasant, and stimulating, was gone.

New people were here. We missed the old. Rather than think of them individually, I am tempted to roll them all up into one representative outsized personality who, to me, stood for the values and temperament of that time. I am thinking of Jack Huntington welcoming the guests he liked to have around him on the broad porch of his tall Victorian cottage beside the tennis courts. At cocktail time, he was an expansive host standing there in joyous expectation as one approached. No sooner had one climbed the steps to the porch than with hearty laughter, he impressed on one an overly generous drink. He was not one to stint on hospitality. The stimulus of the conversation was equally strong. Unlike that found at tamer, more ordinary Fenwick parties, it was not preoccupied merely with local events and gossip. An architect in Hartford, he was deeply involved in the city's cultural life, a key backer of the Hartford Stage Company, but equally, with his music- and art-minded wife, Patsy, a supporter of the Hartford Symphony and of the Wadsworth Atheneum. In a Republican community, they stood forth proudly as Democrats. He had served a term as mayor of West Hartford. Jack was a man of the world and a man of many worlds. A great bear of a man, with a large head and a large body, he seemed to me a Chaucerian figure with lusty appetites and many earthy tales to tell. He made me feel fortunate to be in Fenwick and part of his circle.

My impending leave-taking of Fenwick and the hope of having something to fall back on in late years led me to things I could do on my own without regard to time and place. In London during the Second World War, I had done some drawing in my free time with a friend at an art school out in Hammersmith. It was enough to make me think of returning to it many years later when a friend told me about some informal classes being taught by a young Israeli painter named Merav. When I began working with her in December 1991, Merav was all of twenty-four but already an accomplished painter with schooling behind her and an air of authority beyond her years. She had a small studio in the rear basement of a tenement building in Leroy Street in Greenwich Village, a quiet street only a few blocks long that originated at the busy shopping thoroughfare of Bleecker Street.

We had once-a-week sessions. I can see Merav as teacher looking over our shoulders and pointing out where a line had gone wrong or counseling us to keep it loose, keep it loose. I remember the absolute silence in the room as we worked, the passing hours made solitary by the quiet jazz coming softly from the cassette player, and the break halfway through when Merav served us coffee, and the group appraisals at the end of the evening.

There were just three of us regularly—Sara, Bill, and me. We met at 7:00 and worked until 9:30 or so in the evening. For that first session, I was the first to arrive and met Merav at the door to her studio. We looked each other over. Her dark hair fell across her eyes. She was darkly handsome and sturdily built, totally at one with herself. Physical strength and vitality were clues to her ambition for us as pupils. She appeared unembarrassed at the discrepancy between her age and mine. I took an instant liking to her.

That first meeting was in December 1991, and she would be gone, although we did not know it then, by the following June, returning to Tel Aviv. With her husband, Amir, a musician and composer, she would go home to care for her ailing mother who within a year was to die of cancer.

Knowing her departure was inevitable, she hurried us along in our lessons, taking us from still life drawing to working with a live model, moving from charcoal into oil paint and imposing upon each lesson some added challenge. Once we were given outsize brushes and told to make a painting using only that one brush. Another time, we painted in candlelight. At our last session, we found the easels turned away and were instructed to paint with our backs to the model. Each of us was given a different surface to work with. I was handed a plywood block. When we had finished that last night and held our work up for discussion, she said, "This is some of the best work you have done, and I am not surprised. Each of you had a difficulty to overcome. You had to find a way to get around the obstacle, and in doing so, you tried harder, and out of it came good work. There is a lesson in this for you. Try to put an obstacle between you and the work. Don't always make it easy. And see what happens."

And, nodding her head until the hair fell over her eyes, she added, "I am very pleased with this work."

At that last class, we said our good-byes. To the point of grief, I was conscious of losing, after only six months, one of the best teachers I ever had in any field. But Merav had put me on a path, and I found ways to keep going.

It was almost a year after our offering letter to Fenwick residents went out that the house was officially put on the market and then another fifteen months before we received a serious offer. It was from Anthony Autorino, a Hartford-based businessman with wide-ranging interests that frequently caused controversy and landed him, along with his generous benefactions, in the newspaper. His interest required some negotiation—he wanted the lot combined with the house—before a contract was reached in September 1995. The closing came the following January, which sent nearly $850,000 into my bank account to hold for a year before the capital gains tax had to be met. The balance of the $1,150,000 sale price went to my children for their share of the back lot, which we had valued at $340,000.

In the days and weeks after we'd reached an agreement and before the closing in January 1996, I began to have recurring dreams of a particular character. They came one after the other, each very similar to, or a variation of, the one before. In his discussion of dreams, Freud speaks of anxiety dreams and dreams of wish fulfillment. Mine were dreams of anxiety. I would imagine myself in the cottage once again. All the furniture would be there as if I had not relinquished possession. The new owners might suddenly show up and find the house still filled with the furniture I had contractually promised to remove.

After the January closing, my dreams continued. Sometimes, I would have moved in for the weekend. The house was unaccountably empty and seemed to be ours for the taking. But at any moment, their cars might appear in the driveway. Such dreams persisted for many months.

Through the cottage windows, since early childhood, I had looked out at the world. Two more generations of my family followed. Safe within its shingled walls, they and I were embraced and protected by family. I do not think back upon my own life there without thinking of my parents. They are not with me in New York. They are alive to me in Fenwick.

In the same year in which we sold our cottage in Fenwick, Aalholm in Denmark went out of the hands of the Raben family. Aalholm was sold to a secretive Danish millionaire to satisfy the debts of its last owner. We had the Fenwick cottage for seventy-five years. Once a royal castle, Aalholm had belonged to members of the Raben family since 1725.

No member of Stuzie's side of the family had been able to regard the old castle with any proprietary feelings for all the years it had been in the hands of Johann Otto Raben, known on her side of the family as "the wicked uncle." At least it remained under the family name with all the family furnishings, trophies, and paintings intact within its walls. Now all that was about to go. Johann Otto had died in 1992, and Aalholm had passed to his favored son Johnny. Whatever else may be said about the father, he had been a shrewd manager. His classic car museum, known throughout Europe, was a successful tourist attraction helping to bring some 50,000 paying visitors to Aalholm each year since 1972 when the castle was opened to the public. This was a considerable contribution to the upkeep of a very large property, which consisted of not only the castle and its lands but also some large satellite houses as well.

The appalling mismanagement of the estate by the son and the rapid accumulation of his debts resulted in the dissolution of everything. Those debts were rumored to total some thirty-five million dollars, a good part of it due to wild currency speculation in Russian rubles. As the life of Aalholm unraveled, Johnny Raben thrashed about wildly entertaining a series of ever more foolhardy schemes, at one point even proposing that this once stout old fortress guarding southern Denmark be made available for mass Japanese weddings. Learning of this scheme, Stuzie's nephew Paul Raben said that even if the entire population of Yokohama were to be married at Aalholm, it wouldn't make much of a dent in the debt. The buyer of Aalholm, showing consideration for the family's feelings, expressed no wish to retain the Raben family belongings. The contents of the house were put up for auction.

Paul, the son of Stuzie's late brother Peter, was now the titular head of the Raben family. He was concerned about saving some of the personal household effects and had set aside a sizeable sum of his own money to make this possible. At first, Johnny Raben seemed willing to oblige interested members of the family, but as the auction date drew near, he reneged on his promises in order to squeeze as much as he could out of the property. Paul fought hard to gain a chance prior to the sale to save some of the more important pieces. In the end, he came away with very few. One family treasure he was able to preserve, however, was the portrait of his grandfather, Siegfried Raben, Stuzie's father, by Krøyer, one of Denmark's greatest painters.

Five months after the sale of Aalholm in January 1996, the auction was held. It was conducted by Sotheby's over a four-day period. The lavish preparations celebrated Sotheby's entrance into the Danish market. The nearly two-hundred-page catalogue bore the proud Raben crest on the cover. It was well illustrated with reproductions of rare pieces of furniture, silver and medals, arms and armor, pictures and prints, ceramics and glass, and textiles and linens that Aalholm had in such abundance, collected as it was over nearly three hundred years. In all, there were 2,200 lots. The auction brought between three and four million dollars. Suddenly, only the walls and ancient stones were left. And now, they belonged to an outsider.

It was not a place in which any member of the family wanted to live or that any could afford to keep up. But in Paul's words, "Somehow, one felt that it was the family flagship. The fact that it was not ours was not the point." It was the site of Stuzie's childhood years, of walking hand in hand with her beloved grandfather. There was a loss to be borne, a sense of disconnection, an unmooring of the spirit. The compass no longer pointed in a direction called home.

Chapter 17

Departure

The summer of 1995 was our last summer in the cottage. That fall, in October, we went down to Fenwick for two weeks to wind things up. Only Stuzie and I were in the house, but we expected visits from Suzanne and Christopher to see what they might want of the furniture, the books, and the pictures before we got rid of the rest. Our task was to see that the house was emptied of everything by the January closing, and we had just these allotted days to do it.

Our indoors work did not prevent us from stepping out into the clear October days to walk down the beachfront or get out on the wind-blown golf course to play a few holes. With the summer folk gone and only a few all-year-rounders holed up in their cottages, Fenwick, always brilliant at this time of year, was almost entirely ours. Looking along the roads and fields, we saw no one.

Sunlight flooded the house, warming it by day. The sparkling Sound lay flat and dazzling under the protective lee of the shore, with the fall winds coming out of the north. With the change to Eastern Standard Time, the dark came early, and the nights called for the electric blanket.

The hardest job was deciding what books to dispose of. We would keep the handsome green-bound Temple Shakespeare set, with its engravings and red-ribbon place marker, the Kiplings, and the Charles Reades, but what about the six-volume Carl Sandburg biography of Lincoln? Soon the cardboard book cartons began filling up and dark holes were appearing in the shelves of the bookcase, as conspicuous as empty seats in a theater.

When Suzanne arrived with her companion, Liz Wainstock, we cleared out the sideboard in the dining room of years of accumulated children's games and toys including Suzanne's first doll, given to her by my mother, and the large grey French poodle I had brought her from Paris during my traveling days with NBC in the 1950s. After sorting the books, we were ready for the visit on Thursday of Randy White from the Book Barn down the coast in Niantic. He bent over each shelf, drawing out each book he wanted a careful inch to be gathered up later. He finished in the kitchen, moved to the living room, then to the cases upstairs in the bedrooms, and we were conscious of his footsteps going from bookcase to bookcase. We silently measured how long he lingered at each. He identified our most valuable book as *The River War* by Winston Churchill. Hidden in the shelves for years, it popped up as a total surprise. In the end, he had his haul, some 125 to 130 books out of the 800 or so we had all told, and gave us the calculated worth of the lot. The outcome was welcome, but never so bountiful as one's expectations.

Stuzie began to dig up plants in the garden for possible replanting on our roof in New York. While she was out there, bending over in her familiar gardening posture, I got a call from my friend Anna Crouse in Massachusetts. She applauded Stuzie's raid on the garden and mentioned a similar occurrence in her family when her daughter Lindsay dug up her garden in Vermont and took some of it away before leaving the property to David Mamet, her estranged playwright husband.

The irony of Stuzie's action lay, however, in the utter disregard of the new owners for any of her lovingly tended gardens—not the flower garden behind the front hedge, not the vegetable garden on the west side of the house, not the asparagus bed in front of it, not the raspberry plot alongside the lattice laundry-yard enclosure. They were all obliterated as our buyer Autorino raised the land and elevated the house.

Saturday came, and now we had just four more days to complete the job of clearing out the house. We were in search now of a local antique or auction house that would take what remained of the household furnishings off our hands. The cottage was nothing if not simply decorated, and we had not in our generation added any value to what already existed. What pieces we had could be classified as antique solely on the basis of age, hardly on the basis of beauty or historical value.

My sister Virginia and my brother-in-law Charlie arrived at five o'clock. Nothing very much was left for them to look over, but Stuzie offered sheets, towels, and blankets. The linen cupboard was emptied into black plastic bags and carried to their station wagon, not so much for their own use as for possible sale at a church bazaar. That evening, we went to dinner together at my brother Ted's house in Old Saybrook.

On Christopher's trips to Fenwick from Colebrook, it was difficult to read his expectations and possibly his anxieties. Perhaps for our sake, he kept them to himself. We ourselves could hardly wait to get this job behind us. Removed pictures left blank spaces in the walls like the empty shelves in the kitchen bookcase. The living room looked bare. The long twin rag rugs Christopher's wife, Betsy, had woven for the house were rolled up and carried to Christopher's car. The house was being emptied of its meaning for us.

We got in touch with an antique-collecting firm in Old Lyme. At ten o'clock Monday morning, Judith Enman and her son Brett arrived. After the family had picked over everything, I felt what remained looked pretty forlorn. Nothing troubled the Enmans. They excluded nothing—not that outsized sofa, not the old set of Britannica with crumbling leather bindings, not the piano with broken keys.

On Monday, we sent six boxes of books off to the Acton Library in Old Saybrook. All the pictures were down, boxed, and ready to go. The end was in sight. That night, our friends Julia Ann and Bill Walton asked us to dinner. We had a quiet evening exchanging stories about winter trips we had made and, of course, indulging in Fenwick gossip. That was our last social event from the old cottage.

Thursday, we would be closing up and leaving for New York. Just a few days were left, and the hollow house was somehow chilling in its emptiness. Christopher was with us again, and Wednesday we picked up the

Persky-Hertz ten-foot truck we had ordered to take our stuff back to New York. It wasn't too much—the two handsome Hitchcock chairs, which looked so out of place among Fenwick's makeshift summer furniture, boxes of books, my mother's long Italian bench with her prize-winning needlepoint covering the seat.

So we packed up the truck and prepared to shut the door. I had one last errand to perform. I had saved out the model of our sailboat *Shadow*, that prized relic of my Fenwick boyhood. It was not in good repair. The boom had been broken in an accident, and some of the rigging had rotted away from age.

I carried the model up the backstairs to the dusty attic. It too had been cleaned out. Gone were the discarded shutters, old rusted bedsteads and mattresses, the piles of cast-off clothes, stored family scrapbooks, school books, and miscellaneous treasures that had lain there for years. Up in the rafters of the attic, at the north end, in a place I hoped no alien eyes would reach, I set the model of *Shadow* and retreated from the house.

Postscript:
Alive in Fenwick

We found ways to continue our life in Fenwick for a number of years. We rented someone's cottage for the months of July or August. Of course, it was not the same. It was not the same as having a place where you could store your clothes year-round, a house whose key you held, a place you could return to on impulse at any season, that lived on when you were away, like a member of the family.

Late in August of the summer of 1997, on a Sunday afternoon, we decided to pay a visit to our friend Dick Hepburn. Now in his middle eighties, Dick was in poor health and had largely confined himself to his third-floor bedroom at the top of the house. No longer could he make visits to us. Invariably, they had been the brightest entertainment of our summers.

It was easy enough for us to see Dick when he was alone in the house. But now, Kate was there too—in residence, so to speak. That spring, she had given up the house she had owned since the 1930s in Turtle Bay in New York and had come to Fenwick to live out her life. She was eighty-eight, the same age that summer as her Fenwick neighbor Jack Davis. Although he complained of a sciatic nerve that was aggravated by exercise, Jack was a stoical New Englander. He continued to play golf almost daily, riding the course in his familiar yellow golf cart.

"It's no darn good for it, it almost always makes it worse," he said of the sciatica, "but I couldn't give up the golf."

Kate, on the other hand, was worn out. Her intimate friends like Robert Whitehead and Anthony Harvey, who respectively had produced plays of hers and directed her films, reported that her memory was failing. Like an athlete late in life, she had fought too many battles, suffered too many bruises. Revering Shaw, the Hepburn family had adopted as its golden rule a quotation from the introduction to *Man and Superman*:

> This is the true joy in life; the being used for a purpose recognized by yourself as a mighty one; the being thoroughly worn out before you are thrown on the scrap heap; the being a force of Nature instead of a feverish selfish little clod of ailments and grievances complaining that the world will not devote itself to making you happy.

Katharine Hepburn had lived out that quotation to the last syllable. Ellsworth Grant, after the death of his wife Marion, visited her regularly. He found her sitting in the living room with an open script in her lap. And the same script, he said, would be there the next time, open to the same page.

By bicycle, we approached the house. On our ride, we met Schuyler Grant, Ellsworth's high-spirited, attractive granddaughter and Kate's grand-niece, and said we wanted to see Dick. Schuyler, who was just coming from the house, encouraged us to go. "They're just hanging out there," she said.

Earlier, we had been to Folly Point on the river at the easternmost end of Fenwick to attend an open house of one of the two new houses put up there within the last year. The two houses occupied rather small sandy lots on the shore of South Cove. Totally dissimilar in architecture, clashing irritably in style, they were uncomfortably jammed together on the narrow sandspit. They testified to the relative impotence of that guardian of our culture and architectural integrity, the Historic District Commission. We went through the house on display remarking on the splendid views across the cove and the river and out to the Sound. And, indeed, on the inside, the house was spectacular.

Through the protective alley of black pines, we biked down the drive to the Hepburn house. Parked in the driveway in front of the entrance, as usual, was the white rented car kept for Kate. Other cars were parked by the garage. One certainly belonged to Virginia, Dick's dear friend and companion for years who customarily left her own house in Old Saybrook to spend the weekend with Dick in Fenwick.

Stuzie wanted to enter through the kitchen door beside the garage, the usual way we called on Dick. But the garage doors were all closed, blocking that entrance. So we went through the front door into the hall, calling out Dick's name. The house was silent. There was no response. On easels in the hall were large aerial photographs of the house and of Fenwick. I looked into the living room. Unlike those long stretches of time when Dick occupied the house alone, with occasional visits from one or another of his four children, the living room showed a caring, almost decorative, hand. Flowers in vases stood on tables; bright throw rugs lay on sofas and chairs. The room was orderly and arranged.

We paused in the hall. Stuzie went off to the right and through the dining room to the kitchen, looking for someone to speak to. Through the hall windows, I noticed three figures silhouetted on the south porch facing the Sound. Their backs were towards me. Each figure appeared to be staring silently out to the water. To the right, a large African-American man was seated motionless. A woman, who later introduced herself as Betty, Kate's nurse-companion, looked straight ahead at the water. In the middle, slumped on the porch sofa, her gaze fixed on the water, was the unmistakable figure of Katharine Hepburn.

I went through the dining room and out to the porch, headed for an encounter that I did not look forward to but which I thought could not be avoided. I always had ambivalent feelings approaching Kate, this great and revered person I had admired for so long. Mixed with the excitement of seeing her was the anxiety of how to handle myself in the brilliance of her presence. Now there was a new apprehension: how to deal with her old age and failing comprehension.

As I approached, the man introduced himself as John when I said my name. He gave me a friendly, welcoming smile. We shook hands, and I went over to Kate. She peered at me through pale but unwavering eyes. I was shocked at the change in her appearance since the last time I had seen her more than a year before. Her gray hair was drawn back tightly. She seemed altogether reduced in size. With no makeup, her face was pale, her complexion mottled, and the light in her face, the brilliance of her smile were gone. She looked quite small on the sofa. Her legs were stretched out before her resting on a footstool.

I bent down to her and said, "It's Stuart Little." She regarded me for a moment in silence as if I'd broken in on some sea reverie. From the small, diminished figure came a strong Hepburn-like retort.

"Stuart Little," she repeated. "What the hell are you doing here?"

One always felt a trespasser on her privacy. Now I seemed reduced to one of those unsuspecting tourists who walked the beach in front of her house only to become targets of her shouted commands to go away.

I said, "I've come to see you and Dick."

"Dick's upstairs," she said in a flat, matter-of-fact voice.

John said he'd go and tell him I was coming, and I saw my way to making my departure. Just then, Stuzie appeared on the porch and went up to Kate, repeating the name for her twice and saying Kate knew her, she was Stuart's wife. Stuzie said we'd just been to see the new house out on the point.

"They've spoiled the point," Kate said in the same flat tone.

Looking out over the lawn for another topic, Stuzie remarked on the decaying hull of the *Buzz*, my old fishing launch which I had given to Dick some twenty-five years before when I no longer wanted to pay the boatyard bills. It had lain there ever since at the edge of the lawn, beached and unused, visibly falling to pieces like a neglected shed on a farm.

"It's like the old days," Kate said. What romantic story she had woven around the old boat, it was impossible to tell. We excused ourselves and went up to the third floor to see Dick.

Virginia welcomed us at the head of the stairs. She embraced Stuzie and then me. Dick was sitting on the edge of his bed. He seemed pleased to see us, but now, unlike all those times past, the conversation was up to us. Dick was eighty-five, and for the last year or so, he had sequestered himself in his disorderly bedroom at the top of the house. Seeing Kate and then

Dick, one was struck by the resemblance of each to their father, a resemblance more striking in old age.

We said we had just come from the house warming on Folly Point and remarked on the great views from every window. Virginia said, "Isn't it awful? To have those views, they have spoiled everyone else's views."

For Dick, we had to explain where we were living in Fenwick this summer. It was hard for him to place us anywhere except in the old cottage. Dick seemed restless in the room. He suggested that we move downstairs and have some tea. He glanced across the room at the thermometer by the door.

"It's 97 degrees," he said. "It's too hot in here."

"Good gracious," said Virginia. "How can you read a thermometer across the room?"

"I can't," Dick said. "I'm guessing." He relished the small joke.

Bulky in his red pajama suit, Dick got up heavily and led the way downstairs. On the kitchen counter was a warm luncheon plate of stew which he addressed more out of habit than desire. He took a few forkfuls and lost interest. John suddenly appeared in the kitchen. I could see that Stuzie did not wish to prolong the visit, but mugs of tea had already been set in front of us along with a plate of sugar cookies. We talked about the summer and the visits of family members. Dick asked after our older children by name.

The visit came to an end. We said we'd be back next summer if we could rent again. Dick and Virginia went with us to the front door. As we passed through, Kate was being helped by Betty to the downstairs bathroom in the small bedroom off the dining room. Outside, Dick and Virginia took seats in chairs beside the front door to watch us bicycle away.

We saw Dick the following summer. During the winter Virginia had died. No one knew whether he had actually comprehended this loss. He had been relocated from the top floor of the house to the downstairs bedroom off the dining room where he could be cared for more easily. Sick-room paraphernalia stood in the room. When we appeared, Dick sat up on the edge of the bed half turned away from us. Deafness had set in, and we had difficulty making ourselves understood. His heart was beginning to fail him. This was the last time we saw him.

We were anxious to have a look at our old house after nearly two years of renovation work at the hands of the new owner. I hated to think at what cost to the nerves of our former next-door neighbors and good friends, Peter and Rosalie Brainard, this work had gone on.

A time was arranged with the new owners for later in the day, and we set off as a family, eight of us in all, including an English guest of Caroline and Jasper's. We crossed the Brainard's back lot, cut through past their garage, and were on the doorstep of our old cottage. It was now so completely transformed that while its overall lines remained the same, it was otherwise no longer recognizable as ours.

Inside, the tongue-and-groove wall paneling had been taken down throughout the house, refinished, and replaced exactly as before. The west porch had been elongated to provide a better view of the lighthouse and furnished in such a way as to obliterate our memories of the place. I was startled to see in the middle of the floor a monkey-like rendition of a midget golfer, or maybe a caddy, in a visor cap. It served, apparently, as a joke footstool. The kitchen, which had been remodeled by our young architect friend Ralph Wolfe and in which all of us took so much pride, was completely torn up and revised. Walking into this new kitchen was disorienting. Seeing the changes made here was more unsettling than anything else about the house.

The renovation was done well in every detail. We thanked the owners for this kind tour. Walking away, I decided that, splendid though it was, this was not a house I would like to live in anymore.

Renting around, we saw Fenwick from a number of different perspectives. In one place, we enjoyed a three-year contract, renewed for another three-year period, which gave us almost a sense of permanence in the community. Finally, our rentals ran out. By this time, our three grandchildren had grown up, settling into lives of their own. However happy they were to return to the summers of their childhood, their minds had moved on.

Eliza, an adventurer, had already traveled to Southeast Asia and Africa while still a student studying animal biology at McGill University in Montreal and afterwards on bird expeditions in the bayous of Louisiana and in central Florida tracing the red-billed woodpecker. Later, she joined an expedition to Suriname in South America to live in the rain forest and study the feeding habits of saki monkeys. There was nothing haphazard or ill thought out about her wanderlust. With that controlled and centered mind of hers, she went about the planning methodically. When for some weeks she lived with us in New York, as we were to discover, she was the most meticulously organized traveler. As the time came for us to clear out the loft after twenty-seven years of living in SoHo and pack up to move to Geer Village, a retirement place in northwest Connecticut, she took charge of Stuzie's wardrobe and layered with care the open suitcases. She was our heaven-sent helper. We never worried over her uncertain future; when the time came, she would know where she was going.

Our grandson Joey was a devoted neighbor for ten years just blocks away in New York. He made a success in the world of banking. Whenever he went away, he would call to say good-bye. He would call again when he returned. He had married April in a gala Fenwick wedding and subsequently was summoned to England by his firm. We would have felt bereft in New York without him but for our relinquishing the loft, selling to the conspicuous betterment of our bank account, and making the committed full-time move to Geer, where Christopher and Betsy were close by.

However busy he was at his desk, Joey always had time for the leisurely grandparental telephone call. King of the tennis courts in Fenwick, he had a robust and busy athletic life, particularly in the year leading up to his challenge to the world's racquets champion. This was one match in several years of virtually unbroken victories that he was to lose, but not by much. His athletic life kept us alternately on edge and full of pride. His father gave him a racquet and a ball early in life, and he took it from there.

Our granddaughter Melissa had given up publishing when she sold the regional city magazine in London she co-founded. Her new job was to care for twin boys, George and Julian. For a number of those summer rentals, we had the several times removed pleasure given to great-grandparents of observing the growth of these boys, later to be joined by the determinedly independent-minded Sam to complete the family. We observed the meticulous parental attention of Melissa and her husband, Gavin, even to providing each child daily with a cooked English breakfast. The parents of the twins were a wonder to watch at work (the four generations fit cozily together in the same summer cottage). On a different level, the devotion of the grandparents, our daughter, Caroline, and son-in-law, Jasper caused us to question retroactively our own diligence when these roles were ours, going back a generation. Jasper was a virtual magnet to his grandchildren. He played chess with his three-year-old grandson Sam ("We play by Sam's rules") as if he were facing Kasparov.

Did our transient Fenwick life make us feel like second-class citizens? One suffered the small, inconsequential omissions most keenly. We were dropped from the annual blue address book that listed only property holders. July occasions such as the annual celebration of the Fourth with its golf tournament and fireworks display went by without our participation, and we only heard accounts of such events from friends in August. Unlike my father, who was a long-term member of the board of burgesses, I had never been part of the governance of Fenwick; now it was out of the question. I don't think any of us indulged in the unrewarding pursuit of trying to detect fancied slights from the rest of the community due to our reduced status of not being property owners. It didn't occur to us that there would be any. But, inevitably, we ourselves looked out at Fenwick through different eyes.

Each of us missed something, small or large. Stuzie mourned the loss of her gardens and the chance conversations over the hedge with our neighbor Rosalie. Caroline remembered calling across the street from her upstairs window to her friend Pooh Brainard to plan their day when they were growing up. For Christopher and Suzanne, the house held the secrets of their earliest memories, and so it did for our grandchildren, Melissa, Jonathan, and Eliza.

Giving up Fenwick was to give up something beyond the cottage itself: the land, the place, and the home. Physical connections are strong, but the bundle of associations that went with Fenwick were now gone—for me, for my children, and for their children, who had lived their early summers in that place.

Aside from the gardens, Stuzie was perhaps less attached to the cottage as home and haven than the rest of us. This seemed odd to me. Fenwick for fifty years had been more her home than any place in Denmark, England, or France. Yet at the prospect of change, any change, she was eager, excited. Something new was ahead.

978-0-595-43938-6
0-595-43938-1

Printed in the United States
137708LV00005B/16/P